SAUCERS

OF THE

ILLUMINATI

Jim Keith
Foreword by Kenn Thomas

Adventures Unlimited Press

Saucers of the Illuminati

Copyright 1999, 2004 by Jim Keith

ISBN: 1-931882-24-X

Adventures Unlimited Press
One Adventures Place
Kempton, Illinois 60946 USA

www.adventuresunlimitedpress.com

SAUCERS

OF THE

ILLUMINATI

Jim Keith

The classification of the constituents of a chaos,
Nothing less here is essayed.
—Herman Melville

Dedicated to Ron and Nancy

Other books by Jim Keith

Mind Control, World Control
Biowarfare In America
Secret and Suppressed
The Octopus (with Kenn Thomas)
Black Helicopters Over America
Casebook On the Men In Black
Mass Control

FOREWORD
by
Kenn Thomas

I remember Jim Keith writing this book. At the time, he was also working on an article for the coming issue of *Steamshovel Press* Jim contributed regularly to the magazine and stayed in phone contact for research help and to chat conspiracy. He mentioned that he was trying to summarize all of his current thinking in a single themed manuscript. The original *Saucers of the Illuminati*, in fact, may have been Jim Keith's last contribution to the zine world. The original book had an 8x10 format, spiral bound and resembled more a magazine than a book. Then, many people who knew Keith at all knew him primarily through his small-circulation "fan" magazines (although it is hard to conceive of a conspiracy/UFO cover up "fan"), *Dharma Combat* being the most well known but certainly not the only example. Zines were the happening means of the parapolitical underground in those pre-internet days and Keith served as the super-celebrity of that scene, broadcasting his charm and humor through self-published photocopied wonders, but also writing letters and doing commentary for similar zines produced by others.

Going through my stack of Keith masterworks recently, I discovered *Notes From The Hangar #1* from the early 1990s. In it, Keith published the rant of one Jason Bishop III, making declarations about humans working side-side with aliens in Dulce, New Mexico. Today it has become quite a familiar story, but at the time it was lore that had yet to reach the pinnacle of its currency in UFO circles. In fact, it was still part of what I see as a "barium meal" of UFO disinformation perpetrated by Air Force intelligence agents partly to drive a man named Paul Bennewitz insane.[1] In *Notes In The Hangar*, Jim presented the rant without edit and included several pages of critical response, declaring that he didn't necessarily believe any of it, but he believed in the importance of having it all discussed.

In *Saucers of the Illuminati*, Keith summarized his understanding of that history in a chapter entitled "MJ-12". That chapter remains one of the most concise and complete reviews of that important episode in the history of the ufological subculture,[2] but at the same time comprises only a portion of what this book has to say. From there *Saucers* expands upon Keith's notions about the arcane and occult forces behind human history.

It was a point of view that developed over time, actually re-doing *Saucers* in 1998 in actual book form and now which resonates as a defining echo of the weirdness of the post-9/11 world, years after Keith has gone on to his reward.[3] As the book covers attests, "as the 21st century approaches, many people suspect that something earth shattering is about to happen..."

On the phone back then with Keith explaining the over-arching view he felt he had captured in this new manuscript, I asked him if he thought he could really find a wider audience for the perspective. Wasn't it a bit obscure for the average reader?

We both had televisions on in the back ground as we spoke, both watching *CBS News*. As Dan Rather segued to the commercial, the newly redesigned CBS logo graphic appeared in the upper left corner of the screen. It was the CBS eye neatly pressed within a pyramid. As a looked in surprise at how much it looked like the backside of a dollar bill, Keith asked, "What was that you were saying about obscure?"

1. Thanks to Peter Dale Scott for this concept. It refers to planted disinformation used by intelligence agents in order to track the blow-back. In the Bennewitz case, this meant various Area 51 stories that emerged as part of the UFO circuit presentations of people like John Lear and Bill Cooper, and had peripheral players such as super-spook Gorden Novel and JFK researcher Lars Hansson.

2. The first book-length treatment of the topic, *The Bennewitz Papers*, written by one of Keith's compadres, Greg Bishop, author of the *Wake Up Down There* anthology, is now pending publication.

3. Keith and I wrote *The Octopus: Secret Government and the Death of Danny Casolaro*, which became a hard-to-find cult classic. It currently enjoys a new edition, with one of three new chapters dealing with Jim Keith's unusual death. Among the many strange dimensions of Keith's passing discussed therein was the appearance of *clostridium* bacteria in the kind of knee surgery that led to his early death. Keith had noted years ago the presence of *clostridium* bacteria in the late 1970s cattle mutilations of New Mexico. *Clostridium* also killed our mutual good friend Ron Bonds, who published the first book edition of *Saucers*.

Kenn Thomas publishes *Steamshovel Press*. POB 210553, St. Louis, MO 63121. Samples issue: $7; four issue subscription, $25. Checks payable to "Kenn Thomas," not *Steamshovel Press*."

Contents

Introduction 9

1. A Process of Decoding 11
2. The Human Factor 16
3. The Mind Manipulators 23
4. Infiltration 33
5. MJ-12 38
6. A Symbolic Odyssey 46
7. Increase of Resolution 53
8. Philip K. Dick and the Illuminati 60
9. The Sirius Connection 70
10. Demons and Adepts 82
11. Occult Espionage 85
12. The Year of Light 97
UFOs at the Edge of Reality 107

The Great Seal of the United States of America freaturing
what some believe to be the symbol of the Illuminati.

Adam Weishaupt, founder of the Bavarian Illuminati.

Introduction

In 1993 a miniscule two hundred copy photocopied "researcher's edition" of my book *Saucers of the Illuminati* was rushed into print, upon my urging, by IllumiNet Press. My purpose for authorizing this informal edition was to get into print certain interesting connections that I had made between occult philosophy, the lore of UFOs, and the totalitarian New World Order - ideas that I had discussed at length with other researchers and that were already twinkling into being in a firmament of articles by some of those worthies. I was a little... paranoid is not the word I seek... concerned that by the time a proper paperback edition of *Saucers* was ushered into being, that I might be accused of plagiarizing myself.

As it turned out, my worry was largely unfounded, and little of what I wrote about in '93 has been grappled with, understood, or even mentioned in the conspiracy or UFO press, much less by the *New York Times*. I take this to be positive proof that I was on the right track.

Actually, my sense is that the ideas in *Saucers* tend to jump disciplines from political conspiracy, to UFOs, to the occult, in an attempt to synthesize the information in each. The researchers in those varied disciplines almost never have any truck with and so are confounded by their adjoining truckstops in arcane research. The Left Hand Path doesn't know what the Vast Right Wing Conspiracy is doing, you might say. But these topics are, at the deepest levels, intertwined and clarify the notions of the others.

Another matter: the ideas in *Saucers of the Illuminati* are dangerous, not to mention extremely weird, and stray very close to Things You Are Not Supposed to Think. In fact, in current polite—read mind controlled—society you are not even supposed to think that there are things that you are not supposed to think... Do you follow?

Since the lightning appearance and disappearance of the researcher's edition of *Saucers* in 1993 copies have been completely unavailable, aside from a pirate edition that was rumored to have been put into print. That unavailability created a few misunderstandings about the book. Some speculated in print and on the Internet that the book was too incendiary, too Politically Incorrect, and that it went so quickly out of print because it was suppressed by the CIA or the Men in Black or somesuch. Those things have been known to happen in the annals of conspiracy research, of course, but not in this case. Simply, when I might have been expanding the text of *Saucers* to a length more appropriate for a paperback, I was doing lots of other things: writing nine other books, chasing the wolf of velvet fortune, things like that.

But I finally got around to the revision in 1998. Now here is the bells and whistles version of *Saucers*, with a lot of material not included in the book's original incarnation. Since the first appearance of the book a great deal in the text has been clarified, and the revised work reflects new theories, new understandings obtained, and an arsenal of new smoking guns. Also included in this edition is the text of "UFOs at the Edge of Reality," a lecture delivered in Atlanta, Georgia in 1995.

I admit it. *Saucers of the Illuminati* is my strangest and most controversial work. That fact has been underlined by the largely uncomprehending and sometimes hostile reviews given to the first edition. The book may also be the most true that I have written.

Hold on to your brains. Maybe the world is ready for this stuff now.

1

A Process of Decoding

Regardless of our experience or research, we seem no closer to finding an answer to the puzzle of the UFOs. These strange craft and their equally strange occupants behave in a manner that seems to contradict physics and logic, appearing and disappearing seemingly at will, dropping curious objects and artifacts (including potatoes and pancakes), mutilating cattle, abducting people and leaving cryptic messages embedded in the brains of their awe-stricken contactees. These activities, these odd messages seem only to compound our confusion as to whom these interlopers on "our" cosmic turf are and what their motives might be.

While many saucer contactees or the variegated cults that have risen around them characterize the visitors they have confronted as angelic "Space Brothers" or advanced elder beings intent on warning humanity away from nuclear proliferation or other humanly-fostered evils, other indications as to the motives of these strangelings in silver ski suits are not so positive. Many individuals claim to have been abducted against their will by aliens in UFOs, and they have reported every kind of bizarre and grisly experience, ranging from mystical enlightenment, to the transmission of apocalyptic messages that they must deliver to mankind, even the implantation of tiny electronic brain devices apparently used for mind control or monitoring, perhaps in the same fashion that earthly ranchers now monitor cattle with under-the-skin electronic implants. Something very strange indeed is going on.

Analyzing the conflicting signals that we have received about the nature of these visitors, it is almost as if we are purposely being misled and befuddled by these mysterious agents, purposely being deceived about the motives behind these visitations, and perhaps even directed in some mysterious transformative operation of which we are not aware.

My own interest in the matter of UFOs is rather personal. Although I have been intensely interested in UFOs and the paranormal since my childhood in the early 1950s, it was not until 1972, in the Los Angeles, California suburb of Upland, that I experienced my own first contact—maybe. I came gradually awake in the middle of the night to find an archetypal grey alien staring in my face from a distance of about one foot. I leaped out of bed and raced into the living room. When I returned to my bedroom, the visitor was nowhere to be found.

I really didn't know what to think about what had happened. Was the experience an hallucination at the edge between dreaming and wakefulness? Was it an actual encounter with an alien presence? Was it a cross-dimensional experience that defied the boundaries of dream and reality? I have never been prone to this sort of nightmare, and have not experienced anything comparable in the intervening twenty-five years.

But there was nothing solid to grasp onto about the event, and so I shunted it into the category of maybe. I more or less forgot about the incident until I read Whitley Streiber's bestselling book *Communion* many years later, and one of the accounts in that book tipped the scale toward categorizing the event as being reality, rather than as a nightmare. In Streiber's book it was noted—coinciding with unnerving accuracy with my own apparent encounter—that the color and skin texture of the alien skin was not grey, but rather a deep blue grey, and that it had the shiny almost wet-seeming texture of plasticine. Here was a coherence with another's alien experience that challenged—fractured—coincidence.

So, while I am perfectly aware of the fact that the U.S. military and others have experimented since at least the early 1950s with aerial craft that fit the description of UFOs, while I also know that the UFO experience has been hoaxed, including by American intelligence agencies and by UFO buffs, and that UFOs and abduction experiences may sometimes be a ruse to conceal mind control operations as described in a number of my books, I also leave the latch string out for other more "alien" interpretations of at least a percentage of UFO events.

One intriguing possibility is that the incident in Upland was one of beamed electronic mind control of the sort I have described in a number of my books. The house where the incident took place was a large hippie/radical commune where any number of anti-Establishment pipedreams were hatched. The strange motley of activists in Technicolor dream coats that came and went from the place at all hours no doubt drew the attention of those who monitor such things.

And so it occurred to me: Was I zapped electronically with the image of an alien? Was it just a byproduct of the chromatic chromosomes so prevalent at the time? I will probably never know. What I do know is that there are depths to the UFO enigma that are not plumbed by most researchers in the field, Horatio.

John Keel, for one, is a pioneering researcher who has been able to peer beyond the simplistic "space beings from another galaxy" device that is the primary stock-in-trade of UFO journalism. Of these strange visitors Keel has said:

> Many flying saucers seem to be nothing more than a disguise for some hidden phenomenon. They are like Trojan horses descending into our forests and farm fields, promising salvation and offering us the splendor of some great super civilization in the sky. While the statuesque long-haired "Venusians" have been chatting benignly with isolated traveling salesmen and farm wives, a multitude of

shimmering lights and metallic disks have been silently busying themselves in the forests of Canada, the outback country of Australia, and the swamps of Michigan.

Other researchers have proclaimed that the motives of the visitors may not be altogether benign. It was the famous UFO researcher Jacques Vallee who coined the term "Messengers of Deception" and he has speculated of the UFOs:

> They are physical objects, the product of a technology, but they are also something else: the tools of a major cultural change. I think UFOs are perpetrating a deception by presenting their so-called occupants as being messengers from outer space, and I suspect there are groups of people on Earth exploiting this deception.

Speaking of the experiences of abductees in *Messengers of Deception*, Vallee surmises:

> It is more likely that they have taken a non-physical trip, controlled and guided by a system that acts on human consciousness (the Soviets use the term "psychotronic" to designate such devices), rather than one that is purely physical. The symbols it uses are engineered to have certain effects.

Vallee also reports, "I believe there is a very real UFO problem. I have also come to believe that it is being manipulated for political ends. And the data suggest that the manipulators may be human beings with a plan for social control."

I concur.

The evidence that I present in this book suggests that our vision has been purposely obscured by what we have been led to believe about the UFO experience, and it is probably not directly being done by insectoid extraterrestrials. Aside from the genuine activity of hoaxers and disinformation agents, at least some of them factually connected to government, there seem to be certain elements of the UFO "message" that appear to be purposely designed to deceive. It appears that it was intended that we should be deluded from the very beginning, and it also appears that there is a definite method to the UFO madness.

To my mind the most sensible, yet least voiced explanation is that some UFO encounters are being staged for an ultimate— and ulterior—purpose. Is it within the realm of possibility that there is a group working behind the scenes to convince us that we are being invaded by space aliens?

In order to understand at least a portion of UFO sightings and their purpose, we need to work on decoding what amounts to their curious "language"—a language pieced together from the strange events and messages of hundreds and thousands of encounters, composed of word and symbol and deed apparently bearing meanings beyond the obvious. We must peer below the surface, the apparency, and furthermore, we must view these strange craft and their occupants in a different manner, in a manner that is perhaps not so different than the "open eyes" that secret societies attribute to their metaphysical initiates.

2

The Human Factor

If you were to assimilate the information contained in a large quantity of current books, motion pictures, and television presentations on the subject of UFOs and UFO abductions, I believe that you would be likely—by weight of the evidence presented—to come to one of three conclusions. That,

(A) we are being invaded by aliens from outer space, or

(B) that a high percentage of the human race is crazy and suffering from hallucinations of little green men or worse, or

(C) you would take an "agnostic" approach undecided on one of the first two possibilities.

I will not discount either of the first two possibilities as being the ultimate explanation of what is going on, however I consider it highly unlikely that you would even suspect, based upon information that is generally available, what I consider to be the most likely origin of this phenomenon. My investigations have shown me that UFO sightings (or at least a significant percentage of same) in all probability are the product of an entirely different *praxis* or control process than either alien invasion or hallucination, and that the parties responsible for the phenomenon have, so far as I can determine, never been named as such.

In preparation for the reality shift that I intend this book to entail, I would like to cite a few instances of UFO abductions that do not entirely fit into the media template as to what these encounters are like. In this fashion I hope to shatter the generalized and predictable nature of what are usually put forth as "characteristic" UFO encounters. This will perhaps open the door for new interpretations.

Bruce Smith probably still regrets having chosen to attend a lecture by Budd Hopkins, reputed expert on alien abduction (who, oddly, never entertains the human quotient in his writings), in New Jersey in 1991. The lecture profoundly affected Mr. Smith (as abduction accounts have affected many others) to the point where he packed up his belongings into his trailer home and headed west. Perhaps Smith felt that New Jersey did not have the requisite privacy that encounters with ufonauts usually require.

Camping in Tesuque, New Mexico, Smith woke up in the middle of the night, sensing that he was being visited by someone. Suddenly his ankles were grabbed by a pair of hands and, while woozily drifting in and out of consciousness, he saw a hazy creature looming in front of him... and, oddly enough, wearing glasses and a white, button-down shirt, the kind that his father had worn, according to Smith.

So far, so bad. Smith was dragged away from his tent and campsite but, still semi-conscious and able to partially grasp what was going on, he was able to see that it wasn't toward the expected glowing saucercraft that he was being carried.

Smith maintains that he was manhandled into a large, dark blue van, with markings identifying it as belonging to the U.S. Navy. After traveling for an hour in the back of the van over winding New Mexico roads, Smith maintains that the van stopped and he was levitated out the back door, and was then carried into a huge building that he believes was a portion of the Los Alamos nuclear laboratory.

Once inside the building, Smith was placed on an examination table while a big-headed "alien" examined him and "gouged" at his eyes with a scalpel. Smith went unconscious again and woke up back at the campsite that he had been abducted from.

These terrifying experiences were uncovered several months later while Smith was under hypnotherapy. Smith concluded from the memories that welled forth under hypnotism that he had been abducted many times in the past, but this seems to have been the only time that it happened in collusion with the U.S. Navy.

One is tempted with this account to believe the stories that we hear of government/alien collaboration in abduction and hideous medical experiments—the sort of stories that John Lear and Bill Cooper used to make hay with on late night talk radio, and which still have some currency with the more excitable end of the UFO hobbyist community—but that is not the only possible explanation for the events that Smith says he endured.

The dark blue van is the obvious sticking point in this abductee's tale. Why, pray tell, would space aliens be driving around in vans in order to abduct people? Mysterious vans of this sort are also reported to have been prevalent during a UFO flap in Montana, with "Smithsonian Institute" emblazoned on the side. Researchers contacting the Institute found that they didn't know anything about the vehicles.

In John Keel's *The Mothman Prophecies*, he describes a similar modus operandi taking place in rural Virginia, at the height of the UFO flap of 1973:

> People up in the back hills had been seeing mysterious unmarked panel trucks which sometimes parked for hours in remote spots. There seemed to be several of these trucks in the area and the rumor was that they belonged to the air force. Men in neat coveralls were seen monkeying with telephone and power lines but no one questioned them...

It is perhaps a gauge of the quality of much UFO research that it is considered a serious possibility that these vans sometimes reported in conjunction with abductions and cattle mutilations (or alternately, the black helicopters that often show up around cattle mutilations) are disguised, shape-morphing extraterrestrial craft.

Strange, but if aliens are involved in all of this—and I have grave doubts that they are—instead of vans, wouldn't the more commonly described Star Trek-like "teleporter beams" as depicted in *Fire From the Sky* be more their speed, much more convenient, and less liable to be discovered? More to the point, when driving vans, would little grey aliens be able to see above the steering wheel?

Perhaps the answer is that the beings driving these vehicles aren't alien at all, or at least not quite so alien as we have been led to think. There is no shortage of available accounts of human beings being unaccountably connected to UFOs in the annals of this research, and "close encounters of the human kind" often take place without any accompanying extraterrestrial-appearing characters being involved in the incidents at all. Statistics compiled by James M. McCampbell in the book *Ufology* show, surprisingly, that over one third of "close encounters of the third kind" that are reported involve contact with UFO occupants who are apparently human.

John Keel is the source of another anecdote:

> One family of seven people swore they had seen a circular object land near a wooded area on Long Island. They stopped their car to watch and were astonished when they saw two figures, normal-human-sized beings, exit through a door in the object as a large black car crossed the field and stopped nearby. The two beings got into the car and it drove off. The object took off quickly and disappeared into the night sky.

Another UFO encounter involved two highly credible women, Betty Cash and Vickie Landrum, and Landrum's young grandson, Colby. The trio were motoring near Dayton, Texas in 1980 when they noticed an unusual moving light in the sky above them. They pulled the car over to the side of the road, and the light approached, hovering at approximately 135 feet in altitude and only a few hundred feet away, until it was so close that it was blinding in intensity. By that time the witnesses were able to perceive that they were viewing some kind of huge aerial craft.

Betty Cash, the driver, got out of the car in order to better view what they could now see was a huge, diamond-shaped craft. Flames shot out of the base of the UFO, and a roaring sound engulfed them. Betty Cash returned to the car, where she found the door handle hot to the touch. The strange aircraft slowly moved away. Then the observers saw the approach of twenty-three large, twin-rotor helicopters (apparently Army Chinooks), that looked as if they were escorting the UFO at a distance of about three-quarters of a mile.

After returning home all three of the witnesses of the strange craft had come down with what was apparently radiation poisoning. Betty Cash, the woman who had exited the car for a better look, suffered the worst case, with headache, loss of hair, eyes swollen shut, and sores on her skin, causing her to be hospitalized for six weeks. Since the incident Cash has also contracted cancer that she attributes to the incident. The other two witnesses suffered lesser degrees of eye inflammation and "radiation burns."

When contacted by Cash and Landrum, the Army responded in typical cover-up fashion. Despite the reports of other witnesses that Army helicopters had been in the area at the time of the UFO sighting, they issued a denial of having taken part in the maneuvers. An independent UFO investigator found a blackened area on the road in the vicinity where the witnesses had observed the UFO and the choppers. Within a few days an unidentified road crew hurried to the location, dug up the portion of the road, and replaced it.

What these and similar accounts seem to say is that UFOs and encounters of the third kind are not always an entirely alien affair, that tabloid television may not have all the answers, and that humans may be involved to some unknown extent in many of these incidents—perhaps in some unknown plan of directed transformation that they are trying to implement. Few, very few, contemporary researchers have made this connection, most of them instead opting for the more-easily-graspable notion that the ufonauts are visitors from nearby star systems. There, leave it at that, they seem to say. What else could they be? There are exceptions in the research community, however. Some prominent investigators such as Jacques Vallee, Martin Cannon, Alex Constantine, and John Judge seem to have entirely abandoned the idea that UFOs are extraterrestrial phenomena, although any alternate hypotheses are rarely hinted at in the mass media. Bogeymen "Greys" from outer space make better press it seems, and there are other reasons.

For the general public, I suspect the possibility that UFOs are controlled in some fashion by humans, for some conspiratorial purpose, is unthinkable. Why? The answer is simple. The public is the victim of a massive propaganda assault where you would be least likely to expect one. There is an almost total media blackout about the possibility that UFOs are anything other than extraterrestrial phenomena.

When humans are mentioned in relation to UFOs it is always in the context of some eldritch and vast science fictional conspiracy that includes government/alien collaboration and secret treaties, underground bases, and macabre scenarios of human-alien vat clonings. The monolith of this unlikely scenario is sustained upon a foundation of no hard evidence whatsoever; odd, since it apparently involves hundreds of thousands of human participants scuttling in the dark underbelly of terrestrial politics and selling out the human race for a place in the sun after the coming alien takeover of Earth.

An additional filter on the truth is that the whole subject of the existence of secret, conspiratorial groups manipulating politics from behind the scenes is treated as a big joke by the media, and as the province of crackpots, as can be readily deduced from the treatment accorded to Oliver Stone's motion picture *JFK*. Six months prior to the release of the film, there was a huge media campaign to discredit the production, along with the whole notion of a conspiracy being involved in the John F. Kennedy assassination. Certainly there is abundant evidence showing that it is almost impossible that Lee Harvey Oswald was the sole individual responsible for the murder of Kennedy, and that the large number of inconsistencies in the government story suggest that a conspiracy is at least possible. But that evidence, so it seems, is irrelevant. There are no political conspiracies, and that's that, chump.

Likewise, against the preponderance of evidence, almost the entirety of UFO literature (including motion pictures and television) assumes that the solution to the enigma of the saucers is, in a sense, already known to us. It is taken for granted that we already know that extraterrestrials from other planets pilot these super-science craft. Perhaps, after all, it serves someone's purpose for the public to believe this way. Perhaps it assists the transformation I have spoken of, a transformation that is taking place all around us.

3

The Mind Manipulators

To understand the motives that might prompt humans to
organize such a massive deception, a mass mind-twisting of this
scope, I believe that we should look outside the literature of
UFOs, consulting the history of other recent and verifiable mass
manipulations and deceptions. If we are attempting to unravel
the secret of the most perplexing mystery of this century, we
should acknowledge that certain segments of mankind, in order
to accomplish their power-hungry plans, have often been happy
to pull a veil over the eyes of (if not put out the eyes of) their
fellows who inhabit this earth.

Since the middle of this century (and very probably before
that) the intelligence agencies of the United States, as well as
other countries, have been involved in covert programs intended
to modify beliefs and behavior—to control the minds of the
population of the world. The rubric "National Security" is
employed by these manipulators as a catch-all shield to veil the
illegal (and definitely immoral) activities of intelligence agencies involved in a welter of Orwellian mindbending programs
such as ARTICHOKE, MKULTRA, and MKDELTA.

Although intelligence agency brainwashing is only very
rarely spoken of in the mass media, this does not reflect on its
prevalence or on the magnitude of its ambitions, which have
involved thousands of programs and billions of dollars of

funding into research on mind alteration and the control of often unwitting victims. Many volumes (although few published by major publishing houses) have been filled with horrendous accounts of brainwashing, electroshock, psychosurgery, drug experimentation, and the experimental injection of hostile bacteria and viruses, all performed by "our" employees, the U.S. military and intelligence agencies.

Walter Bowart in the classic expose *Operation Mind Control* characterizes the purpose of intelligence agencies as being

> ...to take human beings, both citizens of the United States and citizens of friendly and unfriendly nations, and transform them into unthinking, subconsciously programmed "zombies," motivated without their knowledge and against their wills to perform in a variety of ways in which they would not otherwise willingly perform. This is accomplished through the use of various techniques called by various names, including brainwashing, thought reform, behavior modification, hypnosis, and conditioned reflex therapy.

A survey of some of the gothic monuments in the landscape of mind control research include:

The advent of television in the late 1940s has provided a potent mind drug administered to the vast majority of the population. Providing a substitution for actual human life in the modulating and hypnotic electronic flicker of the television tube, studies have been conducted showing that television actually induces a trance state that, with years of watching, becomes permanent. Television is, without a doubt, the most potent societal soporific in the mind control arsenal.

Susan Bryce, writing in *Nexus*, aptly describes what takes place during television watching:

> There is so much information coming at viewers over a short time, that they sit lethargically staring blankly at the screen. This is precisely what you are supposed to do. In this lethargic mode, when people are almost snoozing, more is

taken in subconsciously by the mind. Have you ever wondered why people fall asleep in front of the TV? Viewers become passive recipients, on the treadmill of mindless consumerism, routed endlessly from one shopping center to another, buying, buying, buying. Mass programmed shoppers. Becoming absorbed in the pursuit of media popularized roles or fashions, in the vain hope of becoming loved, respected, rich, socially popular or sexually desirable. Sheep who venerate compulsive neurotic behavior as normal, desirable human contact.

Madness Network News chronicles that:

Between 1953-1967, the CIA paid Ewen Cameron over $18,000 to test LSD, Thorazine, and sensory deprivation on mental patients. Dr. Carl Pfeiffer was paid $25,000 a year by the CIA to drug prisoners with LSD. Dr. Harris Isbell drugged prisoners with LSD for 11 years under CIA auspices. Dr. Louis Jolyon West of UCLA, Dr. Sidney Malitz, Dr. James B. Cattell, Dr. Amadeo Marrazzi, Dr. Paul Hoch, and many other psychiatrists were also on the CIA payroll.

Robert Heath at Tulane University in 1955 was employed by the U.S. Army to combine the administering of LSD with implanted brain electrodes on psychiatric victims.

Between 1952-57 Dr. Paul Hoch at the New York Psychiatric Institute was funded to the tune of $200,000 by the Army, to research mind control by drugging on humans.

Nineteen fifty-six saw the CIA authorizing the use of Bulbocapnine and other drugs on state penitentiary inmates. Bulbocapnine was deemed to be especially useful in inducing catatonic states in which brainwashing and implanting of information or commands could be performed.

In 1961 Dr. W. Fry and Dr. R. Meyers conducted experimentation involving the use of focused ultrasonics to create brain lesions, while in 1963, Dr. Peter Lindstrom at the University of Pittsburgh used sonic beams in the focused destruction of brain tissue—a technique said to have been evolved to replace pre-frontal lobotomies.

One prime notable in mind control is Dr. Jose Delgado who, beginning in the 1950s and funded by Naval Intelligence and the Air Force, among others, crafted the first radio controlled brain implants, what he termed "stimoceivers."

Delgado described the capability of these early, crude stimoceivers in the following terms:

> It is already possible to induce a large variety of responses, from motor effects to emotional reactions and intellectual manifestations, by direct electrical stimulation of the brain. Also, several investigators have learned to identify patterns of electrical activity (which a computer could also recognize) localized in specific areas of the brain and related to determined phenomena such as perception of smells or visual perception of edges and movements. We are advancing rapidly in the pattern recognition of electrical correlates of behavior and in the methodology for two-way radio communication between brains and computers...
>
> The individual is defenseless against direct manipulation of the brain because he is deprived of his most intimate mechanisms of biological reactivity. In experiments, electrical stimulation of appropriate intensity always prevailed over free will; and, for example, flexion of the hand evoked by stimulation of the motor cortex cannot be voluntarily avoided. Destruction of the frontal lobes produced changes in effectiveness which are beyond any personal control.

Delgado's stated purpose in the invention of the stimoceiver was the "master control of human behavior," although after a popular treatment of the subject in his book *Physical Control of the Mind* was released, research into the area of direct electrical stimulation of the brain was rarely referred to again.

In the mid-70s, Dr. Louis Jolyon West, director of the Neuropsychiatric Institute at UCLA, suggested a centralized "violence reduction center" to be created at an abandoned missile base in California, a concept that was greeted with approval by then-Governor Ronald Reagan. West reported in a secret memo that one purpose of the center would be the implementation of brain surgery techniques: "...now by implanting tiny electrodes deep within the brain... [it] is even possible to record bioelectrical changes in the brain of freely moving subjects, through the use of remote monitoring techniques."

At the same time that the military and intelligence agencies were drugging, implanting, and sawing up the brains of their experimental subjects, the nation at large was being stupefied by massive drugging promoted by the so-called medical profession and the media as the answer to their cares.

Peter Schrag in *Mind Control* records that, "by 1975 American physicians were writing 240 million pharmacy prescriptions annually for psychotropic medication for people who were not hospitalized—roughly one for every man, woman and child in the country—enough pills all told to sustain a $1.5 billion industry and to keep every American fully medicated for a month." Since that time the prevalence of pharmaceutical drugging in this country has only increased.

During the 1960s a shift seems to have taken place in emphasis in mind control projects. The U.S. military commissioned a number of experimental projects delving into the use of electromagnetic frequencies for controlling and altering the behavior of subjects. Between 1965 and 1970, Project Pandora researched the effects of low intensity microwaves on the health and psychology of humans. This was at the same time that the American embassy in Moscow was being irradiated by microwaves by the Russians, causing numerous harmful physiological effects in the employees there.

Studying Soviet literature on microwaves for the CIA, Milton Zarat determined, "they believe that the electromagnetic field induced by the microwave environment affects the cell membrane, and this results in an increase of excitability or an increase in the level of excitation of nerve cells. With repeated or continued exposure, the increased excitability leads to a state of exhaustion of the cells of the cerebral cortex."

Eldon Byrd of the Naval Surface Weapons, Office of Non-Lethal Weapons, engaged in research into anti-personnel electronics, described the effects of electromagnetic radiation on the offspring of animals. He spoke of "a drastic degradation of intelligence later in life... couldn't learn easy tasks... indicating a very definite and irreversible damage to the central nervous system of the fetus." Byrd also described experiments in which, "At a certain frequency and power intensity, they could make the animal purr, lay down and roll over."

Even more startling brain control possibilities were researched. A 1976 DIA report suggests that "Sounds and possibly even words which appear to be originating intercranially can be induced by signal modulations at very low power densities."

Anna Keel, in *Full Disclosure* magazine, discusses one such experiment:

> Dr. Sharp, a Pandora [Project] researcher at Walter Reed Army Institute of Research, some of whose work was so secret that the couldn't tell his boss, conducted an experiment in which the human brain has received a message carried to it by microwave transmission. Sharp was able to record spoken words that were modulated on a microwave carrier frequency by an "audiogram," an analog of the words' sound vibrations, and carried into his head in a chamber where he sat.

Dr. James Lin of Wayne State University in his book *Microwave Auditory Effects and Applications* discussed the Sharp experiment and remarked that, "The capability of communicating directly with humans by pulsed microwaves is obviously not limited to the field of therapeutic medicine."

Anna Keel writes:

> What is frightening is that words, transmitted via low density microwaves or radio frequencies, or by other covert

methods, might be used to create influence. For instance, according to a 1984 U.S. House of Representatives report, a large number of stores throughout the country use high frequency transmitted words (above the range of human hearing) to discourage shoplifting. Stealing is reported to be reduced by as much as 80% in some cases. Surely, the CIA and military haven't overlooked such useful technology.

Keel also remarks:

Another indication that the government entertained notions of behavior control through use of fields and sound, is a 1974 research proposal by J.F. Schapitz. To test his theory, his plan was to record EEG correlates induced by various drugs, and then to modulate these biological frequencies on a microwave carrier. Could the same behavioral states be produced by imposing these brain wave frequencies on human subjects? His plan went further and included inducing hypnotic states and using words modulated on a microwave carrier frequency to attempt to covertly condition subjects to perform various acts. The plan as released (through the Freedom of Information Act) seems less part of a careful recipe for influence than Adey's and other DOD scientists' work, and may have been released to mislead by lending an "information beam" science fiction like quality to the work.

In an upcoming chapter we will examine the possible use of an "information beam" employed in a highly science fictional manner.

A 1993 issue of the *Tactical Technology* newsletter reported on the then-current state of Soviet mind control technology:

While visiting Russia in November 1991, Morris [Janet Morris, research director of the U.S. Global Strategy Council, a think tank located in Washington D.C., founded by Ray Cline, previously a deputy director of the CIA] and other members of a team sent to investigate Russian technologies for commercial development were invited to a demonstration of mind control technology. A volunteer from the U.S. team sat down in front of a computer screen as innocuous words flashed across the screen. The volunteer was only required to tell which words he liked and which words he disliked. At the end of the demonstration the Russian staff started revealing the sensitive, innermost thoughts of the volunteer - none of which had been previously discussed.

The recorded message was mixed with what appeared to be white noise or static, so when played back it became indecipherable. Since there were no more volunteers in the U.S. group, the Russians volunteered to go upstairs and let the Americans choose a mental patient for demonstration. The Americans declined the offer.

The Russians told Morris of a demonstration in which a group of workers were outside the hospital working on the grounds. The staff sent an acoustic psycho-correction message via their machine to the workers telling them to put down their tools, knock on the door of the hospital and ask if there was anything else they could do. The workers did exactly that, the Russians said.

The Russians admitted to using this technology for special operations team selection and performance enhancement and to aid their Olympic athletes and an Antarctic exploration team. Unlike lie detectors, this machine can determine when the truth is spoken, according to Morris.

Being an infrasound, very low frequency-type transmission, the acoustic psycho-correction message is transmitted via bone conduction. This means that earplugs will not restrict the message. An entire body protection system would be required to stop reception. The message, according to the Russians, bypasses the conscious level and is acted upon almost immediately. They also say that the messages are acted upon with exposure times of under one minute.

Morris envisions this technology will be miniaturized into a handheld device. Presently the International Healthline Corp. of Richmond, Va., is planning to bring a Russian team of specialists to the U.S. in the near future to further demonstrate the capability...

Trilateral Commission kingpin Zbigniew Brzezinski has nicely summed up the mindset of the brain tinkers in these government-sponsored programs, in between gloating over the wonders of the coming New World Order in his book *Between Two Ages: America's Role in the Technotronic Era*:

> In the technocratic society [that Brzezinski sees as the New Order of society coming into ascendance after Marxism] the trend would seem to be towards the aggregation of the individual support of millions of uncoordinated citizens, easily within the reach of magnetic and attractive personalities effectively exploiting the latest communication techniques to manipulate emotions and control reason.

Could Zbig have been any more straightforward in talking about mind control?

We do know that authoritarian (and often covert) control of society continues unabated, the techniques becoming more finely honed as experimental subjects are utilized by the thousands and then discarded. The populace has been drugged, shocked, irradiated, made ill, manipulated, and even killed in the efforts of the military and intelligence agencies and their psychiatric dupes to devise the most effective and invisible manacles for the containment of members of our "democracy."

Is there any suggestion that this sort of mind programming might have been expanded to incorporate UFO incidents and the public's belief in UFOs to assist in their bamboozling? Whatever the answer, I believe that there is little doubt that such UFO incidents could be simulated in this fashion.

What additional capabilities than those described above, and the perhaps added usage of hallucinogens and hypnosis, along with various "extraterrestrial" stage props, would be required in order to convince an abductee that he had been waylaid by a flying saucer, rather than a dark blue van? I am not suggesting that this is the entirety of the answer to the UFO riddle—but might not mind control experimentation of this sort, conducted with UFO space trappings, comprise a statistically significant part, and might not hoaxing, unusual natural phenomena, and the tendency for many UFO buffs to be extremely gullible account for most of the rest?

Ufologist Otto Binder has said, "At any rate, it would seem that the expanding series of saucer sightings in waves, from 1964 to date, is all building up to a crescendo, as if the saucer men are conditioning earth people in seeing saucers, and gradually forcing even the most recalcitrant scientists and government authorities to realize the sightings are not figments of imagination, but real."

The recent huge, triangular UFO seen by thousands of residents over Arizona is exactly the sort of sighting that cannot be ignored. But why would extraterrestrials have to be, or be interested in, conditioning humans to believe in their existence?

4

Infiltration

Although the forces that appear to dominate UFO research seem to prefer that everyone maintain a "Goshwow! Aliens are among us!" approach that beyond disinformational purposes also serves in marketing to the slack-jawed yokels with underbites, there seem to be certain forces afoot today other than just grey aliens. Although thus far we are only able to evaluate circumstantial evidence of UFOs being connected to human occupants (rather than aliens) and the military, there are a number of accounts of the military attempting to infiltrate public UFO research organizations, apparently in an attempt to monitor and disinform the field, and to delude the public at large on the subject of UFOs. On a number of occasions the UFO field has been infiltrated by military intelligence personnel, and well-known UFO "researchers," possibly even the majority of the prominent ones, have loyalties that seem not to reside with the UFO research community or with the truth.

In the early 1950s H. Marshall Caldwell, then acting as Assistant Director for Scientific Intelligence for the CIA, penned the following memo to CIA Director Walter Smith. Caldwell wrote:

> With world-wide sightings reported, it was found that, up to the time of the investigation, there had been in the Soviet

press no report or comment, even satirical, on flying saucers, though Gromyko had made one humorous mention of the subject. With a State-controlled press, this could result only from an official policy decision. The question, therefore, arises as to whether or not these sightings:
(1) could be controlled
(2) could be predicted, and
(3) could be used from a psychological warfare point of view either offensively or defensively.

The public concerns with the phenomena, which is reflected both in the United States press and in the pressure of inquiry upon the Air Force, indicates that a fair proportion of our population is mentally conditioned to the acceptance of the incredible. In this fact lies the potential for the touching-off of mass hysteria and panic... A study should be instituted to determine what, if any utilization could be made of these phenomena by United States psychological warfare planners...

In the book *Clear Intent*, authors Fawcett and Greenwood detail the destruction of the early civilian UFO investigative group, the National Investigations Committee on Aerial Phenomena (NICAP), by government intelligence agents. They cite the involvement in the group of Nicholas de Rochefort, a member of the Psychological Warfare Staff of the CIA, Vice Admiral Roscoe Hillenkoetter, a director of the CIA, and Bernard J.O. Carvalho, another apparent CIA asset.

They describe the removal of Donald Keyhoe as NICAP's director in 1969, and point to the actions of chairman of the board Col. Joseph Bryan, former chief of the CIA's Psychological Warfare Staff as being instrumental in Keyhoe's ouster. They also note that John Acuff, the head of the Society of Photographic Scientists and Engineers—connected to Defense Department intelligence units and the CIA—was the man who replaced Keyhoe. Acuff seems to have defanged NICAP, as far as the government was concerned, turning it into a sightings collection group without a trace of its earlier governmentally-critical policy, an approach that eventually drove the organization out of business. Acuff was replaced by Alan Hall, retired from the CIA, with the group eventually being dissolved.

Further investigation of government manipulation of UFO researchers must include a mention of William Moore, the co-author of *The Philadelphia Experiment* and *The Roswell Incident*, as well as editor, until recently, of *Far Out* magazine, published by Larry Flynt of *Hustler* fame. Moore, who continues to be a medium weight popstar of the UFO research field, for reasons which remain unclear to me admitted at the 1989 MUFON Symposium that he had functioned as an agent for members of the U.S. military, reporting on at least one UFO group and involved individuals in exchange for "leaked," allegedly secret government documents about UFOs. To me this is astounding. The only reason I can imagine that Moore might betray his own activities in this way is that he feared that someone else was going to "out" him as working with the government, and he was attempting damage control by his "voluntary" admission.

Other information on Moore involves the matter of UFO researcher Paul Bennewitz. Bennewitz, a self-employed electronics expert, believed that he had discovered alien technology in action at Kirtland Air Force Base in New Mexico, and contacted the military in an attempt to alert them. Bennewitz was apparently fed a series of documents outlining military collaboration with the aliens and other matters that are currently the stock-in-trade of the "Aliens are among us and polluting our vital bodily fluids!" end of the UFO research spectrum.

According to Moore, "[Bennewitz] was the subject of considerable interest on the part of not one, but several government agencies, and [I discovered] they were actively trying to defuse him by pumping as much disinformation through him as he could possibly absorb..."

Moore admits that he knew that Bennewitz was being disinformed by the government—with evidence suggesting that Special Agent Richard Doty was at least partially responsible—but according to his own admission he took no action to disabuse

Bennewitz of the lies that, Moore says, were gradually driving him crazy. Bennewitz got to the point where he believed that aliens were invading his house and poisoning him. He gradually broke down from the disinformational (and perhaps other) attacks, until he was put into a psychiatric hospital. Sergeant Richard Doty, one of Moore's contacts who was involved in the Bennewitz matter, was a special agent with the Air Force Office of Special Investigations at Kirtland Air Force Base in Albuquerque, New Mexico. During the course of his employment with AFOSI he invited Linda Moulton Howe—a well-known investigator of cattle mutilations who oddly never seems to bring up the government connection—to visit him at Kirtland. Once Howe had arrived at the Air Force base, Doty showed her alleged secret documents that seemed to reveal information on crashed alien vehicles and their occupants. According to Howe:

> These pages... contained a summary of this government's retrieval of crashed disks and alien bodies, including a live alien from a crash near Roswell in 1949. The paper said that this extraterrestrial had been taken to Los Alamos National Laboratory, where it had been kept until it died of unknown causes on June 18, 1952. Then the paper summarized some of the information that had been learned from this distinctly alien life form about our planet and its civilization's involvement with this planet. One of the paragraphs said, "All questions and mysteries about the evolution of Homo Sapiens on this planet have been answered, and this project is closed," ...Further, it stated in the paper that these gray extraterrestrials had been personally involved in the genetic manipulation of already evolving primates on this planet, suggesting that Cro-Magnon was the result of genetic manipulation by the gray extraterrestrials.

Another meeting was arranged between Captain Robert Collins, Howe, and John Lear, the UFO "expert" and former employee of the CIA. Lear is the man who has done more than anyone including Bill Cooper to convince the public that aliens are among us, living in huge underground bases, and collaborating with the government to put us all in the vat-prepared soup.

Collins furnished Lear and Howe with more alleged secret documents on the aliens, and mentioned to her that he had worked with William Moore for years.

It also is within the sphere of William Moore's influence that the bogus MJ-12 paper, a faked 1947 presidential "briefing document" on crashed saucers, surfaced.

5

MJ-12

In mid-1987, when UFO buffs first got the MJ-12 document in their hands, many of them thought that they were fondling the Holy Grail of UFO research. This photo reproduction of an eight-page alleged government document is purported to be a preliminary briefing on UFOs for President-elect Eisenhower, released on November 18, 1952 (also officially the first day of the formation of the CIA).

The MJ-12 document was allegedly used to brief Eisenhower by Rear Admiral Roscoe H. Hillenkoetter, said to be a member of Majestic-12, a top secret research team composed of scientists and military men empowered to investigate UFOs. The MJ-12 document claims that in July, 1947, an alien disk craft crashed in Roswell, New Mexico, and that a second craft crashed on the Texas-Mexico border in 1950.

From where did this historic and apparently earth-shaking MJ-12 document originate? In December, 1984, a roll of undeveloped 35mm black and white film was received in the mail in Burbank, California, by Jaime Shandera, a television producer. Shandera has said that the package was postmarked at Albuquerque, New Mexico. The roll of film was developed by Shandera and William Moore, who found photo images of the pages of the MJ-12 document.

The first publication of a portion of the MJ-12 document

appeared in the *London Observer* newspaper, on May 31, 1987. A small portion of the document was printed in an article by Martin Bailey, titled "Close Encounters of an Alien Kind—And Now if You've Read Enough About the Election, Here's News from Another World." The article was reprinted in many American newspapers in the weeks that followed.

According to British UFO researcher Timothy Good, he was the first to publish the complete MJ-12 document, in his book *Above Top Secret*, in May, 1987. Where did Good get his copy? He stated, "I received the document from a CIA source in March of 1987." When queried as to whether the CIA source had anything to do with William Moore, Good responded, "I am sure. Oh, absolutely."

The document was published and re-published in magazines, analyzed, touted as extraterrestrial gospel, decried as a hoax. But it captivated the imaginations of many UFO researchers, and injected life into an ailing UFO research field to a degree that had not been seen since the halcyon days of the 1960s.

For those UFO buffs who are interested in objective evaluation the fact that no original copy of the MJ-12 document is available is only one of the difficulties in proving or disproving its validity. Because of this fact, no evaluation of the authenticity of signatures, paper, or ink can be made.

The document also is suspiciously similar to a description of the one that was shown to Linda Moulton Howe at Kirtland Air Force Base, if a more refined version.

Other details suggest that the document is a hoax. The dating format is a mixed civilian and military style, as for instance in the date, "18, November, 1952." The military format would be 18 November, 1952," lacking the added comma. Single digit dates also have an added zero inserted before them in the MJ-12 document, a practice that did not come into use in the military until the 1970s. As pointed out by debunker Philip J. Klass, in available examples of Hillenkoetter letters and memoranda, the conventional military date format is used.

Also, according to Klass, a Los Angeles document examiner

has determined that the typewriter used to type the MJ-12 document was not available before 1963.

Researcher Kevin Randle points out another significant discrepancy in the MJ-12 document: "The document is constructed as a briefing paper for President-elect Eisenhower, suggesting that Eisenhower had no knowledge of the Roswell crash. The problem is that Eisenhower, as the Army Chief of Staff in July 1947, would have been completely aware of the Roswell crash."

The MJ-12 report does not resemble in style or substance anything else that I have seen originating from the government, and I have examined hundreds of government documents originating from the same period, many of them dealing with UFOs. The document is also not written in typical "bureaucratese," that elusive jargon so valued in government circles.

The main problem with the MJ-12 document for me, however, is that it solves too much, wrapping up too many of the loose ends of the contemporary UFO controversy, and "proving" exactly what most UFO buffs "already know." Little new information is offered on the alleged saucer crashes themselves, which is rather odd given the fact that this constitutes our first clear look inside the "Cosmic Watergate" so touted by Moore, Stanton Friedman, and others. If this in fact is a briefing provided to Eisenhower, then it is a comic book briefing that would have raised far more questions in the President-elect's mind than it answered. The loose ends that are wrapped up in the document also neatly intersect with the specific stated beliefs and investigative involvement of the men most closely associated with the report: Shandera, Moore, Friedman.

After the publication of the MJ-12 briefing documents, another unsigned document was allegedly discovered in the National Archives, dated July 14, 1954. This is a purported memo to General Nathan Twining, Air Force Chief of Staff, from Robert Cutler, Eisenhower's Special Assistant for National Security. This document states, "The President has decided that the MJ-12 SSP briefing should take place during the already scheduled White House meeting of July 16, rather than following it as previously intended." The alleged memo was unsigned, with Cutler's name and title typed at the page bottom. Advocates of the authenticity of the original MJ-12 pages claim that the Cutler memo provides proof positive that the document—and the alleged secret MJ-12 consulting group—was real, while detractors suggest that the memo is just another fake. The authenticity of the Cutler memo, this supposed confirmation, is doubtful. Advocate Stanton Friedman insists that the memo is real because "it was in a classified box in a classified vault," but this only points up Friedman's willingness to overlook the obvious in his anxiety to verify the MJ-12 document. What would have stopped someone from carrying the Cutler memo in with them when examining the supposedly secure box?

Jo Ann Williamson, Chief of the Military Reference Branch, has indicated that "this particular document poses problems" in a number of ways. Williamson points out that it is not typed on government letterhead and does not have a watermark; it does not have a top secret registration number; it is the single document with a notation about MJ-12 in the folder in which it was found; the marking TOP SECRET RESTRICTED INFORMATION attached to it was not used until many years after the Eisenhower administration; and Robert Cutler was traveling in Europe and North Africa on the day the memo was supposedly issued.

Other significant factors, possibly the most significant in the evaluation of the authenticity of the MJ-12 documents and the Cutler memo are the associations of their recipient and primary disseminators. Jaime Shandera, who reportedly received the film containing images of the MJ-12 document, had in 1980 been involved in pre-production for a fictional movie about UFOs with Stanton Friedman and William Moore. Some rash souls have suggested that the production of the MJ-12 document may have been their next fictional foray. Shandera had also "been working closely with Bill Moore and myself on the Roswell crash," according to Friedman.

Shandera and Moore had both been in contact with Richard

Doty, who was at the time of the MJ-12 document's release working for the Air Force Office of Special Investigations. Doty was trained in disinformation and psychological warfare, and allegedly a self-admitted member of a disinformation group. According to published reports, Moore has stated that Doty reported to a Pentagon official named Hennessey, reportedly chief of security for the Stealth project. It is impossible to gauge Doty's actual connections, since portions of his service records are censored, although while stationed at Linsay Air Force Base in West Germany, according to Klass:

> Doty was charged with falsifying official documents and telling falsehoods to his commanding officer. A formal investigation confirmed these charges and Doty was "decertified" as a special agent [with the] Air Force Office of Special Investigations and returned to Kirtland AFB in late 1986. Doty spent his last two years before retirement in food services management.

Doty was allegedly involved in an earlier UFO hoax regarding a sighting near Kirtland Air Force Base in 1980. An anonymous letter, purporting to be from an airman and indicating that the same information had been submitted to the Office of Special Investigations, was sent to a UFO organization. According to researcher Robert Hastings, "careful analysis of the anonymous letter reveals that it was almost certainly typed on the same typewriter used by Doty..."

According to Dr. Bruce Maccabee of the Fund for UFO Research, Doty also confessed to William Moore that he had been involved in another hoaxed UFO incident, called the Ellsworth case, and that he had forged documents and submitted them to researchers as authentic.

Was Doty or the OSI the source of the MJ-12 documents? Did he forge them? No conclusive proof exists.

But the plot continues to thicken. Researcher Lee Graham has reportedly said that William Moore had contacted him "in an intelligence capacity" and that he worked for the government in releasing sensitive UFO information. According to Graham, Moore had flashed a Defense Investigation Service badge, although Stanton Friedman in his 1996 MJ-12 apologia titled *Top Secret/Majic* puts a different spin on the event. Friedman says, "As a joke, Bill once pulled out a MUFON identification card, flashed it at Lee, and indicated that he was working for the government. Lee bought it." This sidesteps the issue of this alleged impersonation of a government official, as well as Graham's memory of a government badge, not a MUFON card. Friedman carefully sidesteps these matters in his defense of a person who has otherwise admitted to collaborating with agents of the government!

Another issue that Friedman does not approach in *Top Secret/Majic* is Moore's association with men claiming to be Air Force intelligence. Although I was not present at the 1989 MUFON Conference at which William Moore spoke, Jacques Vallee was, and offered the following description:

> In a confused and embarrassing presentation before the MUFON Conference, Bill Moore indeed confessed that he had willingly allowed himself to be used by various people claiming to act on behalf of Air Force Intelligence and that he had knowingly disseminated disinformation, although he has never been "on the payroll." This is a mere play on words, of course. Not being on the payroll does not mean that he was not paid in cash or through other means...
> Moore gave a weak excuse for his actions, claiming that he had acted in a heroic private effort to infiltrate and ultimately expose the operation.

Does Friedman avoid bringing up these matters because they provide additional evidence that the MJ-12 document is a hoax, or simply because he is Moore's friend? It is impossible to know, although Friedman's recent career as a "UFO expert" has been largely based on protesting too much about the discrepancies in MJ-12.

Although the MJ-12 document has not been conclusively

proven to be a fake, the weight of evidence suggests that this is the case. More significantly, to be given serious consideration, in order to be factored in as valid data into any real evaluation of the nature of UFOs, it must be proven to be real, and this certainly has not taken place.

In a sense, it doesn't matter if the MJ-12 document or the Cutler memo are proven to be counterfeit, since the majority of UFO true believers will continue to believe what they want, despite any facts to the contrary. My experience is that a significant portion of the UFO hobbyist community use their obsession as a form of excitement, for the feeling of being "in the know," and as a substitute for a life. Deep down, they hope that we are being invaded by evil aliens!

That aside, it is obvious that the government is attempting to defuse UFO investigations by overwhelming them with incendiary disinformation and by having informants report on the activities of groups and individuals. This is no longer the matter of conjecture that has buzzed among UFO researchers since the earliest days of these investigations. Now there is more than enough proof to show that this is the case.

Providing more support for the idea that UFO abductions may have more to do with humans than aliens, we do know that the American government, at least, is in possession of top secret aircraft of a radically different type than orthodox aircraft, and that these may include saucer craft. Certainly there is much evidence to show that advanced disk craft designs confiscated from the Germans after World War II may have been put into production.

It is only in recent years that the existence of this kind of aircraft has been able to be fairly easily verified by observation outside the military installation known as Area 51 in Nevada. Before this sort of testing moved on to other regions, large crowds would gather outside this military preserve for UFO watching parties. There, on many nights (Wednesday was said to be the most active night for the flights), one was able to observe strange aircraft doing aerial maneuvers that would have been impossible for the unclassified aircraft of which we are aware. But that does not make these craft extraterrestrial, nor does it make them extraterrestrial/human technological hybrids. It does make it obvious, however, that the people who maintain that this is the case, without a shred of hard evidence, are blithering idiots.

The relatively common occurrence of garden variety humans being seen in the vicinity of, entering and leaving, and sometimes piloting UFOs may be another significant clue as to the meaning and origin of these craft. Many operations which are said to take place inside the saucers and performed by "alien" beings are in fact carbon copies of the kind of operations performed on the restraining tables of psychiatrists in the employ of the CIA and other military and intelligence agencies—right down to the reports of tiny electronic brain implants inserted through the nose, the standard insertion technique for both brain control shrinks (as exemplified by Dr. Jose Delgado, the originator of the technique) and, so we are told, the grey aliens.

6

A Symbolic Odyssey

It has been established, I think, that there are aspects of the
UFO mystery that owe more to the activities of humans than
extraterrestrials. But my purpose is not simply to show that
humans forces of some sort—perhaps the CIA—are hoaxing the
populace into believing that the aliens are here and pose a threat
to the well-being of mankind. I am hoping to provide a look into
the purpose behind the hoaxing.

There are strange clues that need to be examined in detail;
these involve a tangled web of symbolism in the UFO mythos
that, fortunately, resolves into a single meaning: Trust me on
this. As I cite each reference in this symbolic odyssey, I will try
to distill the relevant images that will assist in forming a
conclusion.

In the incredible account "My Life Depends On You!",
which has circulated widely in the underground press, Martti
Koski describes the experience of literally going mad. In 1975
he began to be plagued by unwanted voices that he believed were
being broadcast from the hotel room above him. Assuming that
he was experiencing a neurotic bout he put up with the voices
until, in the late summer of 1979, his mental torture escalated.
Now Koski found that he was losing control of his bodily
functions, and that his senses were being scrambled. His heart-

beat became erratic to the point that he entered the University of Alberta Hospital in Edmonton, Canada.

Once checked into the hospital, the voice in his head identified itself, claiming to be a spokesman for the Royal Canadian Mounted Police, and telling Koski that he had been chosen to be a spy. The voice dubbed Koski the "Microwave Man." Koski claims that while in the hospital bizarre experiments were performed on him by the doctors while, in the meantime, interior voices were telling him to perform acts like stealing shirts and engaging in covert sales of cigarettes to other patients.

After leaving the hospital, Koski attempted to escape the barrage of voices by traveling to his native Finland, but to no avail. The voices did not let up.

After eighteen years of psychic attack, Koski has, to a degree, learned to live with it. In Finland he works with other individuals who claim that they have been victims of government mind control experimentation, some of them being able to back up their claims with x-rays that seem to show tiny mushroom-shaped brain implants.

Koski's plight may be interpreted in at least two ways. He may be simply crazy, and the voices may be entirely the product of his own mind. The lucidness of his written account of his ordeal, however, argues against this possibility. He may also be correct in his conclusions. He may be mind controlled by, as he suspects, the RCMP. Certainly there is a huge body of literature detailing the activities of government intelligence operations on civilians, and there is proof that brain implants in fact actually are performed, including numerous x-ray photos of tiny, otherwise unexplainable brain implants. It is also interesting that the most infamous of doctors working in the CIA MKULTRA mind control experiments of the 1950s was Dr. Ewen Cameron, his horrendous experimentation performed at his gothic Ravenscrag facility in Montreal, Canada.

But there is an additional strange element to the Koski story that may provide a piece to the puzzle that we are researching. After Koski returned to Finland, the voices he was hearing began to tell him a different story. Now they told him that they weren't RCMP, at all. They were beings from the "Dog Star," Sirius. So Koski is being mind-manipulated by extraterrestrials?

There are further symbolic linkages on this speculative trail that may or may not lead to the stars. At the beginning of this century, contact with the Sirius star system was claimed by the occultist Lucien-Francois Jean-Maine who, through the famous occultist Papus, learned the rituals of the Ordo Templi Orientis lodge, founded by Aleister Crowley, and formed his own group in his native Haiti. Jean-Maine is said to have in 1922 combined the OTO rituals with voodoo practices to form the Cult of the Black Snake in Haiti. He also claimed to be in contact with a disembodied being or voodoo loa named Lam, an entity who OTO Grand Master Kenneth Grant said was one of the Great Old Ones, an elder as well as eldritch god nigh-identical with those portrayed by the American horror writer H.P. Lovecraft in the 1920s and 30s.

Lam, according to Grant, has the task of uniting the current that emanates from the Andromeda galaxy with the current that flows from Sirius. Grant believed that a dimensional portal exists in the Andromeda galaxy, and through this portal will enter the Old Ones, demonic entities intent on returning Earth to their dominion and having humanity for breakfast.

Prior to Jean-Maine's contact with Lam, the famous occultist and founder of the OTO Aleister Crowley reported that he had summoned the same entity through one of his own "magickal" workings. Crowley also penned a drawing of Lam, reprinted in Kenneth Grant's *The Magical Revival*, adding another strange dimension to the now inter-dimensional puzzle.

Crowley portrays the entity Lam as a prototypical big-headed "Gray," i.e. as the picture of modern popular conceptions about what a UFO alien is supposed to look like. Crowley, relates Grant, also "unequivocally identifies his Holy Guardian Angel with Sothis (Sirius), or Set-Isis." The obvious connection here is the significance of Sirius, although the Ordo Templi Orientis lodge, Crowley, and Lam also have their own special relevance. Evaluating this mish-mash of occultism, who would imagine that the telepathic transmissions from Sirius might have something to do with military intelligence? Occult investigator James Shelby Downard, in his wonderful "Sorcery, Sex, Assassination, and the Science of Symbolism" (published in my *Secret and Suppressed* anthology) researches the existence of a Sirius-worship cult that he believes exists at the highest levels of the CIA! He cites as one of their ritual locations the telescope viewing room of the Palomar Observatory in California. There, he says, the adepts of the Sirius-military intelligence cult enact rituals in the telescopically-focused light of the Dog Star, in imitation of the Egyptian priesthood, astral rays bathing the viewing chamber and the participants when the telescope is aimed Sirius-ward.

Utter madness? Tell that to Colonel Michael Aquino of U.S. military intelligence, the admitted head of the satanic Temple of Set, a deity identified in occultism with Sirius. Aquino makes no bones about the fact that he is the head of his offshoot of Anton LaVey's Church of Satan, known to draw many of its leaders from military circles. Again, we see the strange conjunction of Sirius, occultism, and military intelligence.

Another occultist and "spirit channeler," championing the cause of Sirius, the Dog Star, in the 1950s and 60s, was well-known ufologist George Hunt Williamson (the penname for Michel d'Obrenovic). Williamson authored the classic UFO book *Other Tongues—Other Flesh*, an extended treatise on the beneficence of the ufonauts from Sirius, who supposedly provided mankind with civilization in the far distant past.

Williamson treats this theme at length again in his book *Secret Places of the Lion*, extolling the "Goodly Company," the "Star People," the "Children of Light," who "migrated to earth"—the "dark star"—"planet of sorrows"—about eighteen million years ago and have worked ceaselessly and tirelessly in their gigantic task of acting as the Creator's mentors to a backward, fallen race.

Williamson claimed that he had met these benevolent "space friends," and was in fact a member of the group of witnesses who claimed to have seen George Adamski contact a saucer craft and an alien being in the California desert. The alien warned him about the evil influence of the beings from Orion.

Williamson also rhapsodizes at length, but in a somewhat circumspect fashion, on the seemingly-unrelated theme of Solomon's Temple and the reappearance of the Messiah, hinting at certain "secrets" relating to same. Although it may seem like quite a digression, Williamson's treatment of the Messiah theme provides the solution as to his own and to others' "secret" orientation in ufology.

Drawing upon a selection of quotes from his book, Williamson maintains that:

> Throughout the entire history of the earth, the "Goodly Company" or the multitude of "Christ Souls" have incarnated in a group...
> Pharoah was addressed as "The King, the Ra, the Sun." This signified his position as leader of the "Goodly Company" of star born beings dedicated to the salvation of a planet!...
> A special hereditary order of men was now created to keep a semblance of Aton (One God) worship amongst the Israelites; although the Greater Light could not be theirs because they were not yet ready for it, a less spiritual worship was set up, based on pagan ritualism, that nevertheless was symbolic in its sacrifices, ceremonies, vestments, etc...
> The promise of an Eternal King, to arise out of David's Family, was repeated over and over again: to David, to Solomon, and again and again...
> There are references to the breaking of the bread and drinking of the wine as a symbol of "the sacred repast." The wine represents the "Holy Vine of David" and the bread "the life and knowledge of God." Those "Children of the Greater Light" who are descendants of the "Holy Vine of David"

serve, through the "sacred repast," "the life and knowledge of God!! God made a covenant with David of an eternal dynasty."...
David and Bathsheba prepared the way for the coming of the Master or the Fulfillment in Israel...
When Solomon ascended the throne of his father, he consecrated his life to the erection of a temple to God and a palace for the kings of Israel. David's faithful friend, Hiram, King of Tyre, hearing that a son of David sat upon the throne of Israel, sent messages of congratulation and offers of assistance to the new ruler...
Now we are entering the "twilight of the gods," when the final destruction of the Old Age will take place and man and the gods will be regenerated and reunited! Man will have revealed unto him a true vision of his eternal heritage—that earthly things may show him the nature of his spirit!

So sayeth George Hunt Williamson. But what do the Temple of Solomon, Hiram, King of Tyre, the "Holy Vine of David," the ancient manipulation of Earthlings by space aliens, and the coming "Fulfillment in Israel" have to do with Sirius, the Dog Star? A surprisingly large amount, it turns out.

A more recent version of essentially the same Sirius scenario is provided by the UFO contactee Oscar Magocsi.

After contact with the extraterrestrials, Magocsi believes that he has a mission to impart the wisdom of the "Psycheans," members of the "Interdimensional Federation of Free Worlds," whose base of operations is located near Arcturus. Magocsi reports that humanity migrated from the Pleiades thousands of years ago, and that we (and the Interdimensional Federation) are at war against evil forces from Draconis. These Dark Forces, Magocsi maintains, rely on human allies—the Illuminati secret society—whose mission is to assist in enslaving mankind through a long term disinformation operation intended to portray them as forces of good hailing from the Orion nebula. There are, Magocsi claims, actual good guys from Orion—he dubs this faction the Lords of Light—but the Illuminati are a different bunch altogether. Magocsi also maintains that a particular area of positive influence is Sirius, the intelligences there supposedly beaming telepathic transmissions intended to counteract the bad vibes of the Dark Forces.

7

Increase of Resolution

A few additional notes need to be added to this mystic cacophony before a conclusion can be drawn about Sirius, the Temple of Solomon, and the nature of UFOs. A remarkable UFO group was contacted by Jacques Vallee in Paris, France. The group is called the Order of Melchizadek, and it uses the Star of David for its emblem, and for its program espouses a one world government and the doing away with money and religion—except for the UFO-oriented sort of religion, I would imagine. The Order is cabalistic in its mystical practices, the Qabalah being an ancient form of Jewish mystical cosmology, a philosophy also employed by other occult groups such as the OTO and the Freemasons. Vallee notes the curious number of organizations that the head of the French Order of Melchizadek fronts, including the Front for Christian Liberation, Jesus People Europe, Jesus Revolution, the Charismatic Christian, the Christian Socialist Party, and Jew and Arab movements. Here relevant cross-currents include cabalism, the Order of Melchizadek, and the Star of David. Throw in one world government and the abolition of money and religion for good measure.

Another French UFO group that Vallee investigated should be stirred into the melange. The Frenchman Claude Vorilhon was taking a pleasant hike in the mountains one day—so he relates—when he saw a UFO hovering nearby, the craft bearing a Star of David with a swastika inside the emblem. A glowing childlike figure stepped forth from the craft. The child conversed with Vorilhon, bestowing a new name on him, "Rael," and informing the man that the reason he had been chosen to be contacted was because France was the birthplace of earthly democracy during the French Revolution. The being entrusted Vorilhon with the mission of building an embassy in which the aliens, which Vorilhon calls the Elohim, from the biblical reference, could meet with dignitaries of Earth, with the stated task of spreading "Peace, Love and Fraternity."

Vorilhon was informed that humans had been created by the Elohim, godlike space travelers who were also skilled in the arts of DNA alteration and cloning. Vorilhon was now to assist the Elohim in preparing mankind for the final age of Revelation.

Vorilhon, now going by the name Rael, insists to his numerous followers that "A world government and a new monetary system must be created. A single language will serve to unify the planet."

He and his followers now sport the Star of David/swastika that he observed on the side of the UFO, and practice a form of "sensual meditation" that may be similar to kundalini yoga as practiced by the OTO and other groups.

Of the Rael cult, Jacques Vallee observes:

> The most remarkable facts about Rael-Vorhilon are that he has acquired a large number of disciples—including thousands of followers in French Canada—and that the cult seems to have sources of income beyond the donations from his flock, leading some to speculate that the Raelian movement... like Jim Jones' People's Temple, may have attracted the attention of social engineers motivated by the observation and management of such belief systems.

An additional case, that of Betty Andreasson, should serve to link this twisted chain of incidents.

Andreasson's abduction was the subject of a book by Raymond Fowler, titled *The Andreasson Affair*. Although her case has been discussed at great length in the UFO-related press, and has been the subject of a number of television segments, no one has satisfactorily explained the extremely strange nature of the events she experienced, ones that are quite different from typical UFO abduction events, as least as they are usually presented. Taking place in 1967, the events of Betty Andreasson's abduction were later brought out through the use of hypnosis. Andreasson recalled being kidnapped from her home and spirited away into what appeared to be a spacecraft. She was transported to an unknown location and then taken through a series of underground passageways that she believed were part of a city. Arriving at an underground chamber, Andreasson experienced, in a manner that she describes as highly painful as well as emotional, a kind of mythic psychodrama enacted before here which may not have been different from the kind of mystical dramatizations enacted in ancient Mystery Religions and other mystic cults.

She saw a huge bird, that she estimated to be fifteen feet in height, resembling an eagle but with a more elongated neck. The creature was apparently alive, but as Andreasson watched it, it began to transform. It began to glow with a light and heat that was so intense as to cause her pain. When the heat and light had diminished the bird was gone and she was gazing on a pile of flickering embers.

As Andreasson stared at the embers she saw a worm wriggling in the ash. "Now, looks like a worm," she described it during her hypnosis, "a big fat worm. It just looks like a big fat worm—a big gray worm just lying there."

Also during the experience, Andreasson was told by her abductors, "We are going to measure you for light... You have not completely understood the word that you have. You are not completely filled with light."

She said, "I believe I am filled with the light! I believe—I believe that I'm filled with the light!"

Andreasson also recalled that, "They called my name, and

repeated it again in a louder voice. I said, 'No, I don't understand what this is all about, why I'm even here.'
"And they—whatever it was—said 'I have chosen you.'
"'For what have you chosen me?'
"'I have chosen you to show the world.'
"'Are you God?' Andreasson asked, 'Are you the Lord God?'
"'I shall show you as your time goes by.'"
The following text is part of an interview with Betty Andreasson, conducted by Raymond Fowler:

> FOWLER: Have they [the UFOs] anything to do with what we call the second coming of Christ?
> ANDREASSON: They definitely do.
> FOWLER: When is this going to occur?
> ANDREASSON: It is not for them to tell you.
> FOWLER: Do they know?
> ANDREASSON: They know the Master is getting ready, and very close.

Since we are ranging cosmically far afield in our search for connections, it should be noted that Eye in the Triangle emblems have been seen on some UFOs and the uniforms of their occupants, that Men in Black sometimes wear the same emblem and speak of themselves as being members of the "Nation of the Third Eye," and that in recent years a significant percentage among 2,000 UFO sighting reports in Belgium describe triangular craft with lights at each point of the triangle, and another light in the center of the triangle. This may be the same gigantic aircraft seen over Phoenix, Arizona in 1997—again, the Phoenix!—a craft identified as being a UFO in the news media, but conforming to descriptions of top secret aircraft currently being produced by the military.

To reiterate the elements I have been stirring together in this and the preceding chapter: the "Dog Star," Sirius—the "Lords of Light" and various other references relating to light—the Eye in the Triangle—the Illuminati—Set—Isis—the Temple of

Solomon, the Star of David, and God's reported covenant with Israel—the Qabalah—and the Phoenix. All of these symbols convey a single Earthly origin.

Is it surprising to note that these are the symbols and catchphrases of a secret society that has existed since—conservatively—at least the 1700s, and which draws upon mythology that began with the Egyptians, if not earlier. That society is the Illuminati, whose most visible proponents currently are the Freemasons, a secretive fraternal order with many members among the ranks of prominent world leaders, politicians, intelligence and military, and with conclaves located in virtually all towns of any size in America. Although the vast majority of Freemasons know very little of such arcane imagery and purposes, the information is there to be perused in their books and in the performance of their mystical initiatory rites.

Albert Pike, the head of the Scottish Rite of Freemasonry in the 1800s, announced that, "Sirius still glitters in our Lodges as the Blazing Star *(l'Etoile Flamboyante)."* He also spilled the symbolic beans when he said that Sirius was interchangeable with the Eye in the Triangle, the Mother Goddess Isis, and the pentagram beloved of many a mystical sect.

One of the secrets, perhaps the core secret of the Illuminati and of their related societies (including the Freemasons and the Priory of Sion secret society as revealed and simultaneously concealed in Baigent, Lincoln, and Leigh's seminal *Holy Blood, Holy Grail*) is that the overall goal of this secret society is the rebuilding of the destroyed Temple of Solomon in Jerusalem.

The secret within the secret is that this is the purpose of the New World Order (another Illuminati conception), namely the enthronement of a new Messiah from the genetic line purported to descend from King David (and Jesus, thus fulfilling the ambitions of both Jews and Christians) who will rule over the world in feudal fashion and supposedly usher in a new era of transcendent wonderfulness.

Gibberish? The Freemason Pike said in the 1800s: "Behold our object, the end, the result, of the great speculations—of antiquity; the ultimate annihilation of evil, and restoration of Man to his first estate, by a Redeemer, a Masayah, a Christos, the incarnate Word, Reason, or Power of Deity." When Freemasons tell you that the group is all about performing good works and driving around in funny little cars on the fourth of July, don't believe them. They have a metaphysical agenda, although only those initiated at the highest levels are aware of it.

This agenda is exactly what George Hunt Willamson is getting at when he talks about the "Holy Vine of [King] David": a physical bloodline of individuals descended from the alleged marriage of Jesus and Mary Magdalene, and from King David. This scenario is also a key to the battle plan of the New World Order (whose agenda seems to go back, in this instance, to at least the time of the Knights Templar).

So UFO celebrity George Hunt Williamson had it, and so the varied branches of the Illuminati have it, although in highly cryptic fashion. If it is thought that Williamson is merely echoing biblical themes and in fact had no secret Masonic orientation woven into his writings on UFO contact, we should listen further to his words:

"Solomon," Williamson says, "was a great artist; he designed most of the burnishings for his Temple of God. He was an alchemist, and manufactured by alchemical means the gold used in his Temple. The transmutation of base metals into gold was accomplished by 'vibrations.' Alchemy was more than a speculative art—it was also an operative art!" Similar, perhaps, to the speculative and operative lodges of Freemasonry?

The Andreasson encounter reiterates a number of secret society symbols, including its familiar 'light' motif, but centers around the explicitly Masonic symbolism of the death and rebirth of the phoenix. In the informative book *The New World Order,* Ralph Epperson asserts, "The phoenix bird symbolizes a rebirth, not only of an individual inside the Masonic religion but also of a new civilization arising out of the ashes of the ruined one."

And this appears to be the plan of the Illuminati.

In recent years the highest levels of political manipulation have been directed toward fulfilling the biblical prophecy and Freemasonic philosophic cornerstone of rebuilding the Temple of Solomon in Jerusalem on the site of the Dome of the Rock, a Muslim holy place, and placing a World King of Davidic bloodline on its throne. There have been several attempts by terrorists linked to high level Israeli intelligence to blow up the Dome of the Rock, the reported site of Solomon's Temple, an event which is rightly seen as a certain motive for the launching of a holy war between the Jews and Arabs.

Making it even more likely that the Dome of the Rock will be destroyed, and the Temple of Solomon rebuilt is that a red heifer has been born in Israel—supposedly the first red heifer since the destruction of the Second Temple by the Romans in A.D. 70. The ashes of a red heifer were traditionally used for purification before approaching the Holy Temple. Some Muslims are concerned that the birth of the red heifer will be seen as the signal for the destruction of the Dome of the Rock.

"The potential harm from this heifer is far greater than the destructive properties of a regular terrorist bomb," David Landau wrote in the Israeli newspaper *Ha'aretz*.

As far as the possibility that the recapturing of the reported site of Solomon's Temple will set off war, and possibly nuclear war in the Middle East, not many Jewish or fundamentalist Christian sects—or even Freemasons—are likely to be much worried about this possibility. Millions of dollars have in fact been channeled into the terrorist organizations from Christians in the United States in their fanaticism and belief that the rebuilding of Solomon's Temple will set off the advent of the Messiah, which conveniently also carries all the earmarks needed for it to parallel the second coming of Christ.

And the manipulation continues...

8

Philip K. Dick and the Illuminati

The most revelatory account I have come across of a possible contact with an alien intelligence is the book *VALIS* by Philip K. Dick. Aspects of the book that seem to be little understood are symbols that point to an encounter of some sort with what we can accurately term the Illuminati. Again, the messages in *VALIS* are coded, and the meanings encoded are Freemasonic, comprising in fact a relatively exhaustive recapitulation of Freemasonic lore and agenda.

VALIS is a semi-fictionalized account of "Horselover Fat," Dick's alter ego (the name formulated from a word derivation of his name), and Dick's meeting with what he takes to be God, or at least a God, via the medium of a pink beam of light. Dick dubs this god VALIS (a Vast Active Living Intelligence System).

Dick's vision came about when, in March of 1974, and suffering from two impacted wisdom teeth, he waited in his apartment in Anaheim, California for a prescribed pain killed from a local pharmacy. When the delivery person from the pharmacy arrived at the door it was a young woman wearing a golden fish-emblem necklace. Dick reflects that:

For some reason I was hypnotized by the gleaming golden

fish; I forgot my pain, forgot the medication, forgot why the girl was there. I just kept staring at the fish sign.

"What does that mean?" I asked her.

The girl touched the glimmering golden fish with her hand and said, "This is a sign worn by the early Christians." She then gave me the package of medication.

In that instant, as I stared at the gleaming fish sign and heard her words, I suddenly experienced what I later learned is called anamnesis—a Greek word meaning, literally, "loss of forgetfulness." I remembered who I was and where I was. In an instant, in the twinkling of an eye, it all came back to me. And not only could I remember it but I could see it. The girl was a secret Christian and so was I. We lived in fear of detection by the Romans. We had to communicate in cryptic signs. She had just told me all this, and it was true.

This sudden influx of knowledge had been caused by a pink beam of light that had shot out of the necklace the girl was wearing, the beam apparently penetrating directly into Dick's head and imparting a vast array of information, including the knowledge of several languages that he had not previously understood. Aside from feeling a sort of hyper-rationality, Dick sensed that he had been taken over by a superior mind that had memories dating back in excess of two thousand years.

Later Dick was to hear troubling, grotesque messages coming out of his radio telling him to die, and would have an all-night display of graphic inner vision similar to thousands of abstract paintings seen in rapid succession projected upon the mind's eye. He also experienced a superimposition of the features of ancient Rome onto those of the California landscape in the 1970s, and formed the conviction that the present world was locked in what he termed a "Black Iron Prison," a state of spiritual (and probably physical) entrapment.

From these experiences and others Dick evolved a complex body of speculation, from which he drew a trio of books that included *VALIS* and a lengthy *Exegesis* consisting of several thousand pages of handwritten notes speculating on the nature of his contact with what he determined to be God.

The outcome of Dick's experiences with VALIS was not altogether benign. After the encounter (and a breakup with his wife) Dick attempted to kill himself, ending up in a mental ward instead. What Dick believed to be the source of his contact is particularly interesting:

> "Where did the plasmate [VALIS] originally come from?"
> After a pause Fat said, "From another star system."
> "You wish to identify that star system?"
> "Sirius," Fat said.

In *VALIS* Dick relates the fairly widely-known information on the African Dogon tribe and their startling and unexplainable exact astronomical knowledge about the Sirius star system (as described in *The Sirius Mystery* by Robert G.K. Temple—possibly a pseudonym?). The Dogon, Dick says, "got their cosmogony and cosmology directly from the three-eyed invaders who visited long ago. The three-eyed invaders are mute and deaf and telepathic, could not breathe our atmosphere, had the elongated misshapen skull of Ikhnaton and emanated from a planet in the star-system Sirius. Although they had no hands, but had instead, pincer claws such as a crab has, they were great builders."

Dick has Horselover Fat dreaming of these three-eyed creatures: "They manifested themselves as cyborg entities: wrapped up in glass bubbles staggering under masses of technological gear... Soviet technicians could be seen, hurrying to repair malfunctions of the sophisticated technological communications apparatus enclosing the three-eyed people." I will have more to say about the Dogon later in this text.

Dick also believed that, "Our world is still secretly ruled by the hidden race descended from Ikhnaton, and his knowledge is the information of the Macro-Mind itself... From Ikhnaton this knowledge passed to Moses, and from Moses to Elijah, the

Immortal Man, who became Christ. But underneath all the names there is only one Immortal Man, and we are that man." "Real Time ceased in 70 C.E.," Dick asserted, "with the fall of the Temple at Jerusalem [i.e. the Temple of Solomon]. It began again in 1974. The intervening period was a perfect spurious interpolation aping the creation of the Mind. 'The Empire never ended,' but in 1974 a cypher was sent out as a signal that the Age of Iron was over; the cypher consisted of two words: KING FELIX, which refers to the Happy (or Rightful) King.

"The two-word cypher signal KING FELIX was not intended for human beings but for the descendants of Ikhnaton, the three-eyed race which, in secret, exists with us."

Dick believed that, "The person referred to by the two-word cypher KING FELIX is the fifth Savior who... VALIS had said, was either already born or would soon be."

Out of the VALIS communications, "Fat deduced that he had a mission, that the plasmate's invasion of him represented its intention to employ him for its benign purposes."

Of Ikhnaton's three-eyed kin, Dick alter-ego Fat observes, "My God... These are the original builders...," to which another character replies, "We have never stopped... We still build. We built this world, this space-time matrix." This is reminiscent of the terms with which the Freemasons refer to themselves in such tomes as Pike's *Morals and Dogma*. There is no mistaking the connection for anyone with the slightest familiarity with Masonic lore.

And VALIS, we learn, employs the same mystical communication system as the Masons: "All its verbal information is stored as Cabala." The Qabalah (alternative spelling, Cabala) is an ancient form of mysticism that pervades Freemasonry, top of pyramid to base.

Dick describes the method by which VALIS initiates secretly communicate with each other: "During a handshake, a motion with one finger of two intersecting arcs: swift expression of the fish symbol, which no one beyond the two persons involved could discern.'' The connection with the secret handshake of the Freemasons is obvious.

In *Exegesis,* Dick amplified on his beliefs:

> For the first time I have inferential evidence that a genuine secret fraternity of authentic Xtians exists, & has affected history... & possess supernatural powers & Immortality, due to direct links back to Christ—so they are the true hidden church. The two historic interventions which I am sure of collate: the secret fraternity fights the Empire (Rome in all its manifestations) & promotes the evolution of man to higher levels by inner & outer regeneration. The 16th, 17th century Illuminati are connected with this secret brotherhood...

Whether the godlike VALIS was involved at all, what was communicated to Dick seems to be approximately what the Freemasons and their brethren want us to believe about their mission: that theirs is an ancient tradition resting on an immortal bloodline that comes from the star system of Sirius, and that the fulfillment of their plans (including the rebuilding of the Temple of Solomon, and the enthronement of a World King (their secret agenda hidden in their convoluted inner circle cant) is the only salvation for this soon-to-be One World.

Dick seems to believe that VALIS took the form of a satellite, firing electronic beams of information down upon the Earth. Or perhaps crop circles? He has one of his characters say, ''The satellite had control of them from the get-go. It could make them see what it wanted them to see... The satellite has occluded them, all of them. The whole fucking United States.''

There are other indications that the actual VALIS that Dick contacted may have come from another source than Sirius. ''In Fat's [i.e. Dick's] opinion, his apartment had been saturated with high levels of radiation of some kind.''

He theorized that, ''the Rosicrucians [the philosophic precursors to the Masons] were telepathically beaming pictures at him, probably boosted by micro-relay systems of an advanced order;

but then, when Kandinsky paintings began to harass him, he recalled that the main art museum at Leningrad specialized in just such nonobjective moderns, and he decided that the Soviets were attempting telepathically to contact him.'' Later Dick theoretically pinpointed the transmissions as originating from the schemes of a crippled rock musician named Mini: "He visited the Soviet Union one time; he said he wanted to see certain experiments they were conducting with microwave information transfer over long distances.''

Fat himself comes to believe within the pages of *VALIS* that, "All that was involved from the start... was advanced laser technology. Mini found a way to transmit information by laser beam, using human brains as transducers without the need for an electronic interface. The Russians can do the same thing. Microwaves can be used as well. In March 1974 I must have intercepted one of Mini's transmissions by accident; it irradiated me.''

Actually, I doubt that Dick felt the source of his infernal "enlightenment"—that happened to him in real life, in much the same fashion as it was depicted in the partially fiction *VALIS*, as shown by his statements in his Exegesis—was a rock musician. It happens that information beam experiments of exactly the type that Dick speculated on were at about that time being conducted by both the CIA and the KGB.

CIA Director Richard Helms described research taking place in the 1960s into "sophisticated approaches to the 'coding' of information for transmittal to population targets in the 'battle for the minds of men'" as well as "an approach integrating biological, social and physical-mathematical research in attempts... to control behavior." He described "use of modern information theory, automata theory, and feedback concepts... for a technology for controlling behavior... using information inputs as causative agents.''

Anna Keel, in *Full Disclosure* magazine, writes:

Due to [the CIA's] Project Pandora, it is now known that

applied biological (and other) frequencies can also be used as direct "information inputs" (e.g. of feeling or emotion) and to reinforce brain rhythms associated with conditioning and information processing. One way to get such a signal into a human may be through use of a high frequency carrier frequency. Results of research into information processing, unconscious processes, decision making, memory processes and evoked brain potentials would likely be exploited or integrated in an interdisciplinary system.

For difficult subscribers... there are substances that have psychological or psychobiological effects ranging from subtle through devastating, and that cause increased susceptibility to conditioning. Some of these substances are similar to ones which are recognized by neurotoxicologists or behavioral toxicologists as occupational hazards; some are variations of substances used experimentally in laboratories to produce selective damage in certain neuronal tracts. Many substances needn't be injected or orally ingested, as they may be inhaled or applied with "skin transferal agents," i.e. chemicals like the popular industrial solvent dimethylsulphoxide (DMSO), which can, in fact, enhance the applied substance's effect. For instance, some compounds cause damage that produces increased sensitivity to stimulus, distraction (or flooding of thought associations), and enhance susceptibility to influence i.e., a state where automatic parallel information processing, which usually takes place outside of awareness, and interferes with conscious or more intentional limited channel processing. While causing acute mental symptoms wouldn't be the goal in groups, producing mild distraction, an ego weakened blurring between the sense of "I" and "you," would enhance some kinds of conditioning and promote suggestibility; then, perhaps transmitted "thought associations," "the voice of God," "lucky advice" or whatever, can more easily get through and have an effect... Convenient to the agencies involved in covert influence, is that among primary symptoms of schizophrenia or mental illness are ideas that one is being influenced by "transmissions" (e.g. radio frequencies), "voices" or even telepathy; unless complaints about covert psychological weapons are well organized, they would tend to be discounted as indicative of mental imbalance.

Another approach that may have been used is the transmission of "key concepts" to matters that the subject is already conversant in, creating a realignment of the subject's sense of reality by the injection of just a few bits of information, images, or sentences. In Dick's case this might have involved accessing his study of religious symbolism and history. A fast acting hallucinogen and a beamed transmission of religious concepts might have made him very susceptible to the idea that, due to an unexplainable event of "gnosis" he had tapped into the secrets of reality.

Dick describes a message broadcast "Out over the airwaves by one of the largest TV stations in the world, NBC's Los Angeles outlet, reaching many thousands of children with this split-second information which would be processed by the right hemispheres of their brains; received and stored and perhaps decoded, below the threshold of consciousness where many things lay slumbering and stored." He terms the message the KING FELIX cypher, and reports that, "The United States Army cryptographers studied it but couldn't discern who it was intended for or what it meant."

Dick describes the way in which the message was broadcast:

> On the screen the words FOOD KING appeared—and then they cut instantly, rushing their film along as fast as possible so as to squeeze in as many commercial messages as possible; what came next was a Felix the Cat cartoon... One moment FOOD KING appeared on the screen and then almost instantly the words—also in huge letters—FELIX THE CAT. There it had been, the juxtaposed cypher, and in the proper order: KING FELIX.

I don't know whether the KING FELIX cypher or the Food King/Felix the Cat messages were actually broadcast (other than in *VALIS*, that is), but discounting the possibility out-of-hand would be unwise. Certainly similar messages have been sent over the airwaves, such as the Eye in the Triangle station break presented by CBS during 1992. A perfectly clear representation of the Eye in the Triangle was shown, quickly metamorphosizing into abstract patterns. Curious as to whether I was projecting my own fixations, I polled an audience of about a hundred people from the podium at a UFO convention; the majority of them had also noticed the depiction.

Another television subliminal was the image of the Statue of Liberty projected between the film frames of an ALF cartoon, as reported in *TV Guide*. Surely that image must have been slipped into the programming by some overzealous right wing patriot skulking in the CBS editing room. So one would tend to believe, but check out what conspiracy theorist and Freemasonic expert Norma Cox has to say in her *Secrets* newsletter on the subject of Lady Liberty:

> [This] is the statue of the Moon Goddess, Diana... This Queen of Heaven is also the Queen of Democracy... Diana's right arm holds a great torch (symbolizing the sun) high in the air. The left arm (right and left symbolic of male and female), grasps a tablet which bears the date of the Declaration of Independence. A crown with huge spikes, like sun rays, rests on her head (the crown covertly represents our satellite, the Moon)... Note the similarity between Juno, holding aloft a sword and Diana, whose statue, symbolizing Freedom, Equality and Worldwide Brotherhood, stands in New York harbor. Worshipped as Juno Lucina, the Bringer of Light, Illuminism's adoration of this Moon goddess ranks only slightly below that of the god of the Sun who, in the case of Juno, is Jupiter (Zeus), her husband.

I have been following examples of the injection of occult symbolism via other conduits; one of these, amazingly, impossibly, is Camel cigarette advertising. Although the media has been hip to the idea that the cigarette company is specifically targeting young people with their cartoon "Joe the Camel" cigarette campaign, no one that I know of has spotted the fact that the Camel ads are riddled with subliminal imagery, including occultist subliminal content. It begins with the Camel image itself, the camel being a symbol of Isis according to Aleister Crowley. Other images I have noted in these ads are the obviously phallic snout of Joe the Camel (this representation has been noted by other, including mainstream writers), the phallus being a seminal occultist obsession; a tiny representation of a man with erect phallus on the cigarette package's front; and a sprinkling of other important occult symbols such as the rose, the moon, the ocean, the eye in the triangle, and the pyramid, all Isis or Illuminati symbols, prominently featured for no apparent reason in Camel advertising. There is even a depiction in one ad of Joe the Camel as George Washington; is it possible that Robert Anton Wilson and Robert Shea were on to something in their *Illuminatus!* trilogy, when they suggested that George Washington was impersonated by Adam Weishaupt, after the suppression of the Bavarian Illuminati, and that this is the significance of this ad? Nah.

But to return to Philip K. Dick... Ultimately the VALIS enigma is difficult to interpret with any absolute sense of certainty about what took place that day in March of 1974. It shines with points of illumination whose meaning remains elusive against the explanations of prosaic reality. What we do know is that, for whatever reason, in whatever fashion, Philip Dick had almost the entire Illuminist/Freemasonic mythos fired into his forebrain, and that he struggled with those images, trying to make sense of their symbolism, for the short period of time that remained in his life. Either he was force-fed a massive injection of Freemasonic mythology via electronic beam (as he believed), or in a moment of dreadful illumination—or perhaps hallucinogenic receptivity—Philip K. Dick saw the truth of the world.

9

The Sirius Connection

The Freemasons tell a very curious story about the origin of their order and of civilization. They believe, in a mythology with roots dating back to the time of the Sumerians, that civilization on Earth (not to mention the secret occult doctrine) was established by divine visitors from the star system Sirius, which they symbolically equate with the Egyptian god triunity of Isis, Osiris, and Horus. In the Sumerian mythology they are explicit in stating that these extraterrestrial visitors, who they term Oannes, were fish-like in form. Isis, it may be observed in Egyptian representations, wears a fish headdress. The home system of these alien visitors, the star Sirius, was of such significance to the Egyptians that they based their calendar and the alignment of their temples on the star's rising times.

Harry Lebelson in an essay titled "The Search for Ancient Astronauts" reports the following of the fish-like extraterrestrials:

> The Oannes were described as teachers who gave the people insight into letters, the sciences and art. Referring to cuneiform and pictographic records compiled several thousand years before his time, [the scholar] Berossus describes how the Oannes taught the people to found temples and codify laws; they taught the principles of geometrical

knowledge and 'everything to humanize mankind,' as Berossus put it.

Here is the theme of extraterrestrials visiting Earth thousands of years ago and civilizing it, along with the information that these visitors specifically imparted information on building ("The Builders") and geometrics, orientations central to Freemasonic lore and symbolism.

We do know that, for whatever reason, there was a sudden quantum leap in civilization that took place virtually simultaneously in Sumeria and Egypt. According to Professor W.B. Emery in Archaic Egypt:

> At a period approximately 3400 years before Christ, a great change took place in Egypt, and the country passed rapidly from a state of advanced Neolithic culture with a complex tribal character to two well-organized monarchies, one comprising the Delta area and the other the Nile valley proper. At the same time the art of writing appears, monumental architecture and the arts and crafts developed to an astonishing degree, and all the evidence points to the existence of a well-organized and even luxurious civilization. All this was achieved within a comparatively short period of time, for there appears to be little or no background to these fundamental developments in writing and architecture.

And the reason for this remarkable increase in human knowledge is known to us, although not admitted. Although the truth has not filtered into the hallowed studios of the 6:00 News, it is not in question as to whether mankind has come into contact with an extraterrestrial culture. We have. There is complete confirmation of the legend of the Oannes, which has been obtained in the 20th century. Proof of that contact resides in the secret cosmological traditions of the Dogon tribe of Africa.

The traditions of the Dogon have been transmitted in oral fashion for centuries, and may comprise the most pure offshoot of the secret tradition that underpins the religious beliefs of diverse religions and secret societies - including the Illuminati. Their tradition clarifies the secret agenda of the major occult and religious traditions of this planet. And that pure transmission from the Dogon speaks of, verifies and conclusively proves extraterrestrial contact.

The secret tradition of the Dogon is centered upon the star Sirius, but more significantly, upon its smaller companion Sirius B. The problem is that Sirius B is totally invisible to the naked eye, and was only discovered through the use of a powerful telescope in the 20th century. It might have only been a lucky guess that the Dogon attributed an orbiting companion to Sirius, if only they hadn't made so many more "lucky guesses" that prove their scientific knowledge of the star system:

— They know that Saturn has a ring around it, although it is impossible to determine this fact without the aid of a telescope.

— They are aware that the planets in this solar system orbit around the sun, and that the solar system is contained in the Milky Way.

— The Dogon say that Earth's moon "is dry and dead like dry dead blood."

— They are aware of four moons of Jupiter.

— They know that the Earth turns on its axis.

— They also know, most significantly, that the orbital period of Sirius B around Sirius A is fifty years; again, a fact impossible to determine without a modern telescope.

Where did they obtain this information? They say that they were taught it by intelligent amphibious beings called the Nommo—the term used in both a singular and plural form— who came from Sirius thousands of years ago in a circular, spinning ark. Their tradition is a precise correlation with the Sumerian tradition of the Oannes. The Dogon call the Nommo "the Shaper of the world"—note the similarity to Phil Dick's concept of "the Builders."

The Dogon have a number of interesting things to say about Sirius and the Nommo. During Dogon ceremonies the Sirius system is portrayed on a checkered blanket, recalling the tessellated or checkerboard pattern that the Freemasons favor for their floors: is this a reference to Sirius?

The Bozo tribe, cousins to the Dogon, call Sirius the "Eye Star," a concept hearkening to the Eye in the Triangle and to the Egyptian glyph for Isis' consort Osiris. It is noteworthy that the Bozo say that Sirius A is "seated." Isis is depicted in Egyptian hieroglyphics with a symbol of a seat or throne.

Remarkably, there is another religious tradition on which the lore of the Dogon may cast a penetrating light. The Dogon refer to mankind as Ogo, the imperfect, the outcast. They say that the Ogo were rebellious and were unfinished as a creation. In order to make up for the rebellious—sinful—nature of the Ogo, one of the Nommo, named O Nommo, "Nommo of the Pond," was sacrificially crucified on a tree to atone for our imperfect nature, died, and will return in an ark with the ancestors of men.

According to Robert K.G. Temple in *The Sirius Mystery*:

> The name Nommo comes from a Dogon word linked to the root nomo, "to make one drink." It is said: "The Nommo divided his body among men to feed them; that is why it is also said that as the universe 'had drunk of his body' the Nommo also made men drink. He also gave all his life principles to human beings." He was crucified on a kilena tree which also died and was resurrected.

The helical rising of Sirius was key in Egyptian—as well as Dogon—religious ceremonies. The Dogon also portray the helical rising of Sirius as a cross with a flower-like sun in its center, an image very reminiscent of the flowering cross of the Rosicrucians and their successor groups like the Freemasons and the Ordo Templi Orientis.

It may be speculated that the fish symbol of the secret society that Philip K. Dick felt had contacted him may have derived from the Oannes/Nommo connection. The fish symbol, stood on its head, also portrays a representation of the fertility cult of Isis, and it is even possible that the Christian fish symbol is similarly derived, since it may be argued that Christianity is at core a Mystery Religion of Osiris-Sun God worship, transmogrified by claims of an historical uniqueness that it specifically does not possess.

As Aleister Crowley wrote in *The Book of Thoth*:

> In this card [Death, a Tarot card] the symbol of the fish
> is paramount; the fish (il pesce, as they call him in Naples and
> many other places) and the serpent [symbolizing the Messiah]
> are the two principal objects of worship in cults which taught
> the doctrines of resurrection or re-incarnation. Thus we have
> Oannes and Dagon, fish gods, in western Asia; in many other
> parts of the world are similar cults. Even in Christianity,
> Christ was represented as a fish. The Greek word IXThUS,
> "which means fish, and very aptly symbolizes Christ," as
> Browing reminds one, was supposed to be a notariqon, the
> initials of a sentence meaning "Jesus Christ Son of God,
> Saviour." Nor is it an accident that St. Peter was a fisherman.
> The Gospels, too, are full of miracles involving fish, and the
> fish is sacred to Mercury, because of its cold-bloodedness, its
> swiftness and its brilliance. There is moreover the sexual
> symbolism.

Michael A. Hoffman II in *Secret Societies and Psychological Warfare* observes the following of the star Sirius, that it is, "regarded in the highest occult circles as analogous to the 'hidden god of the cosmos'... The emblem of the All-Seeing Eye above the unfinished pyramid is the representation of the eye of Sirius, of its omniscient surveillance."

An investigation of the beliefs of Freemasonry (and, incidentally, of the other major religions both exo- and esoteric on this planet) shows that this "charitable fraternity" is merely an updated version of ages-old and archetypal Osiris/Isis Sun God/Mother Goddess programming. This form of worship can be traced back to the literal beginning of recorded history, its mythology anciently crystallizing into the Isis/Osiris Sun/Moon cultus of the Egyptian priesthood.

Osiris, it so happens, was one more divine visitor who is claimed to have civilized the backward and mud-rutting people of Earth with his teachings. From Egypt the deities of the Sun pantheon may have taken on different names (including Ra, Odin, Jehovah, and Jesus, with feminine counterparts including Diana, Mary, Ishtar, Rhea, Astarte, Cybele, and Ma), but the mode of worship and populace control was essentially the same. The adepts of the Sun/Moon programming (of which Freemasonry is a major surviving branch) have always called themselves variations on the term "the Illuminati," the origin of the phrase betraying its source. Illuminati—Illumination—the adepts of the Sungod and his consort. When I state this derivation of the term there are no doubt many who will think I am distorting and oversimplifying this religio-occult progression—but I am not.

A quick and cursory sketch of the main branches of the Illuminati might go something like this, although I admit that others might offer a family tree somewhat different in its branchings. This is a secret society, remember, and what we know of the Illuminati has been obtained by accident (as when lightning struck down a member of the Bavarian Illuminati in the late 1700s, providing us with a cache of inner circle documents), or has been eked out through conjecture, inference, and interpretation of their double-talk code language.

In Isis/Osiris veneration, we can see the beginnings of the ritual trappings of the Mystery Religions that were to follow. One reason that the Greek and Roman Mystery Religions are mysterious is that little is known of what actually took place in their rites, celebrated primarily at night and in caves. We do know that Mystery Religions were the source of many of the practices that were taken up by later secret societies including the Freemasons, and that they partook—practices varying somewhat from one Mystery group to the next—of secret ritual initiation involving dramatizations of the lives of the gods, the imbibing of psychedelic drugs such as magic mushrooms, sex orgies (with an emphasis on homosexuality), and at least in some instances, human sacrifice. The symbology of "light" pervades the Mystery Religions, adepts having been said to "have seen the light," "had their eyes opened," and so forth, all very appropriate to celebrants who enacted their rites in the dead of night in caves. Light = Illumination = Illuminati.

From the Mystery Religions, which were extremely influential upon the tenets of Christianity, came the philosophies of the Gnostics, composed of a number of secretive European sects, the most prominent perhaps being the highly secretive, perhaps even fictional, Priory of Sion.

Again, we know very little of what the actual practices of the early Gnostics were, but we do know that the Sun God/Mother Goddess orientation had in certain cases taken on a more philosophical bent, dealing with the eternal cosmic war between darkness and light. Again, the motif of "illumination" is represented. A recent translation of a document of the Cathars, perhaps the most prominent of the Gnostic groups, suggests that one of their secrets was that they were a straightforward Isis cult.

The Jewish/Gnostic mystical practice of the Qabalah, whose origin may have been about the time of Jesus or shortly after, was a primary influence on a number of secret society tributaries, including the Rosicrucians and the Knights Templar. Qabalism was also the singular greatest philosophical influence on the Freemasons, which in the mid-1700s evolved a return to an overt Sun God/Mother Goddess mythology, along with an emphasis in their practices on the importance of the star Sirius. Freemasonry, aside from being an essentially Gnostic religion, has comprised since its inception a vastly important influence in world politics and in world intelligence agencies, and may be the most active and far-reaching of the Illuminati fronts at the present time.

Freemasonry and the Rothschilds international banking group (the Rothschilds being from the beginning of their dynasty Freemasons) were the main influence on diamond magnate and Freemason Cecil Rhodes' Round Table secret society, formed around the turn of this century. Rhodes was the single most important Freemasonic spearhead into world political control.

Currently we may note the Trilateral Commission (with their symbolic "666" triangular emblem and orientation), the Council on Foreign Relations, and the Bilderberger Society as being among the most influential organizations on this planet; these sprung from the Round Table group.

While I am limited in space in this thumbnail sketch, it is very possible to trace the twistings and turnings of the Illuminist philosophy until we encounter the secret Freemasonic rituals of the elitist leaders of today, men like George Bush of the Skull and Bones German Illuminati offshoot, Henry Kissinger and Alexander Haig, alleged to be members of the Freemasonic P-2 group, and in all probability the (Cecil) Rhodes scholar, Trilateralist, and saxophone player from Little Rock, Arkansas, the highly symbolic Masonic location where the arch-Mason Albert Pike formulated his schemes.

Why were the Sun and Moon chosen by the Illuminati of ancient history as deities for the worship of their slaves and underlings? My guess is that it is a relatively arbitrary choice that reflects solar-lunar influence in a simple, understandable fashion, particularly as it might be understood in an agrarian society where these astral bodies are the obvious and all important influences in a people's day-to-day life. If the sun doesn't shed its beneficent rays on the Earth, then the crops don't grow.

There is an additional associative quality of the Sun God/Mother Goddess programming that pertains to the human mother and father and accesses our unexamined and authoritarian-inlaid childhood programming, digging into deeply ingrained programming much in the same way that beer commercials on television access a different level of instinctuality, by being larded with sexual imagery.

As the cult of the Sun God and his consort first evolved, the Illuminati made it well known that they were the chosen representatives of these immortal deities—and did the people REALLY want to take a chance on not believing what they told them? The masses had better treat the Illuminati real nice, or they might have a word with the Sun God and his consort and have them bring a punishing plague of frogs.

"In the beginning," the Sun God and Moon Goddess were in absolute control, working in mysterious and usually sadistic ways that were only fully decipherable to their Illuminated envoys. A lot of people fell for this stuff, and they were probably given little tin badges that clearly identified them to the hold-out heretics whom they in turn tortured and murdered in order to assist them to "see the light."

In time (say about the time of the Chaldeans) the Illuminati started to believe some of their own programming and began to study the movement of the Sun and moon and their brother and sister stars and planets. This gave the Illuminati another leg up, via astronomy, in being able to predict coming occurrences like eclipses and comets. By the time astrology was formulated, the Illuminati had it all pretty well sewn up, with franchises in operation all over the planet.

Science began in a similar fashion as astrology—gasp! But the dominant belief modes of humanity have always been given names like "Science," which simply means "knowing." During the sixteenth century when the noble Illuminati popularized this latest version of "knowing," they had lots of free time to dabble in astrology and alchemy (the forerunner of modern chemistry) and, for a change of pace, to participate in sex orgies in groups with names like the Hell Fire Club.

Since the Sun God (and his various relations, including sons and wives) were, after several thousands years of worship, beginning to fray around the edges in terms of believability, and a lot of commoners were beginning to grumble that this stuff was all made up, the Illuminati came up with a new and improved version of their mind control software that didn't depend upon the Sun God or Moon Goddess for ultimate authority. As the Sun/Moon cult lost some of its popularity, "Scientists" were quick to take up the slack. According to their propaganda, the physical laws of the universe were the ultimate causative factors, and naturally, those physical laws were only fathomable by the scientific (i.e. Illuminati) elite.

Now the Illuminati restored their waning dominance with their promotion of the arcane wisdom of bunsen burners, stupefying Mesmerism and electricity, and they no longer—at least at the present time—needed to draw their powers from mystical associations of the stars and planets. Their vision of the universe and society, as fostered by members of the British Royal Society and other Illuminati-conceived groupings, became the predominant worldview. The main tenet of their new religion, Science, was that whether you understood it or not, it was always Right. Not so different a creed than the programs that preceded it.

The British Royal Society of the late seventeenth century was the forerunner of much of the media manipulation that was to follow. After the re-tooling into "scientific" values was accomplished by the Illuminist masters, society (in the view of the Illuminati) needed to be conditioned for stability in a capitalist and non-religious format. The cogwheels had to be greased. This was accomplished by the launching of non-religious, pro-scientific attitudes through the same media vehicles that influence us today: newspapers and books, with radio, motion pictures and television soon to follow.

And heretics against either Science or Religion have always been dealt with in summary fashion—sometimes possibly in dark blue vans by CIA technicians dressed to look like space aliens.

Now we are in an era—which we arbitrarily term "modern," but which seems to have no claim to that appellation—whose religion is a hybrid of both science and mysticism: this is the religion of the UFO and the New Age. It is a religion that performs the functions of all religion: it induces awe and susceptibility and confusion and guilt and restimulation of infantilism, and opens up the believer to intervention by the priesthood.

Attempting to crack the secret of the nature of this elusive beast, the UFO:

— Isn't it odd that the U.S. military just happened to be working on disk craft back in the 1950s when the whole UFO flap started?

— Isn't it odd that the mind control implants that are supposed to be inserted through the nostrils of UFO abductees just happen to conform exactly to the implants designed by Dr. Jose Delgado, the CIA mind control researcher?

— Isn't it odd that several of the most prominent among "UFO researchers" have been members of military intelligence, men such as John Lear, "formerly" of the CIA?

— And isn't it the oddest thing of all that the intelligence agencies of all countries crawl with Freemasons, and that the CIA just happens to have a reported faction of Mother Goddess cultism within its ranks?

Attempting to get a grip on this topic, why would "UFO" testing be done relatively "out in the open," on military reservations that can be fairly easily observed by a public notified of UFO flights by "former" CIA men eager to spread the truth about the little grey men? Are the military authorities teasing us, as it were, with this open testing, along with all the other revelations of the secret order that underlies the normalized facade of our society and media?

When George Bush spoke repeatedly of the New World Order, is it likely that he would have simply forgotten the thousands of right wingers and conspiracy buffs who for years have used that phrase as the personification of world fascism, evil, and mind control? Or was something else going on, some other process or directed transformation?

When CBS broadcast an Eye in a Triangle in their station identification, could it possibly have been done by accident? Does this not hearken to the "cant" language, the mystical double-talk employed by Freemasons and other secret societies?

Michael Hoffman II has spoken about similar processes involving "revelation of method" or the purposeful giving away of arcane secrets of Freemasonry, which he dubs "the cryptocracy." He likens this to the activities of the alchemists:

This is what simplistic researchers miss: the function of macabre arrogance thumbing its nose at us while we do nothing except spread the tale of their immunity and invincibility further. That is the game plan operant here. To the belief system of the modern man it sounds too crazy. Why would the perpetrators want their secrets revealed after the fact?... This question can only be definitively answered if one has an understanding of the zeitgeist which overseers in the cryptocracy have partly manufactured and partly tailored their own operations to coincide with. As I've pointed out, secrets like this were rarely revealed in the past because traditional people had not yet completed the alchemical processing (of mind control). To make such perverse, modern revelations to an unprocessed, healthy and vigorous population possessed of will, memory, adherence to their deepest inner intuition and intense interest in their own salvation, would not have been a good thing for the cryptocracy. It would have proven fatal to them.

But to reveal these after-the-act secrets in our modern time, to a people who have no memory, no willpower and no interest in their own fate except in so far as it may serve as momentary titillation and entertainment actually strengthens the enslavement of such a people.

There is an occult/Freemasonic stratum in the command structure of media and world control. There is a long-term occult agenda in geopolitics that is just now coming to poisonous fruition.

10

Demons and Adepts

Secret societies such as the Freemasons have been linked throughout their history with the kind of otherworldly visitations that we associate with UFOs, having now conveniently pigeon-holed the phenomenon into a "scientific" categorization that removes them from the relatively discredited earlier pigeonhole of being demonic. "These are highly evolved beings from the planet Xenon," we might be saying, "flying in craft that are thousands of years in advance of our own. You can't use a crucifix to scare these babies off."

Historically many occultists have claimed to channel alien beings that conform exactly to allegedly extraterrestrial visitors that are described today, although in the past this phenomenon was considered to be related to religion. Jacques Bergier, in *Extraterrestrial Visitations from Prehistoric Times to the Present* even credits the possibility that these entities actually exist, suggesting that the proliferation of alchemical, occult, and scientific knowledge that took place in the fifteenth and sixteenth century may have been due to contact with otherworldly beings by Illuminati such as Roger Bacon, Jerome Cardan, and Leonardo da Vinci. Is it possible that during the Middle Ages the Nommos made a return visit?

Bergier attributes the alien influx of knowledge to "Information Source X" and believes that:

This knowledge was connected with alchemy but went beyond it... A knowledge that came from where? More or less directly from those Intelligences who are able to light and extinguish stars at will—an essentially rational knowledge, offered without request for payment and not requiring adherence to any religion—a knowledge that must have filtered over to [Jonathan] Swift, enabling him to predict the Martian moons.

Certainly, during the Middle Ages contact with angels and Men in Black and sundry demons (often dressed in "shining armor") was almost taken for granted by the populace, although I have the suspicion that it was probably in the interests of the clergy and secret mystical societies to play this material up and to weave legends around it. At that time the term "demon" did not always carry the satanic overtones that it does in this era, and the descriptions we have of the otherworldly beings from that time suggest that they were of two general descriptions.

There were the monstrous succubi and tormentors of humans that the clergy—including Catholic, Protestant, and Jewish—got a kick out of spooking their aptly-termed flocks with. There was also the category of entity said to have been in contact with the Illuminati of the day, and that group seems to have been more interested in imparting the advanced and arcane knowledge of alchemy and astrology and science than in forging diabolic pacts and wagering souls.

Note the difference: the clergy would be well-served by the imps of hellfire, while the Illuminati, affirming their possession of transcendent knowledge, would be served by contact with wise, unearthly spirits who didn't have anything to do with the bugaboos of mainstream religion. Not that I am absolutely positive that some of these "demons" may not have been real, but this dual orientation suggests that at least some of them were invented, just as some UFOs are invented.

Bergier quotes Jerome Cardan, who claimed to be in contact with demons: "Just as the intelligence of a man is greater than a dog's, in the same way that of a demon is greater than a man's.''

Bergier also reports:

> During the Middle Ages, appearances of creatures with garments of light were most common. These messengers went to meet rabbis, with whom they held lengthy discussions on the cabala, the powers of gold, the knowledge and exploration of time, etc. They stated that they knew the guardians of the sky, but were not guardians themselves...
>
> There is no law against interpreting this radiance and the demons' shining garments in terms of our twentieth-century mythology, against imagining that the "double face" [displayed by many of the demons] is a space helmet, that the "luminous garment" is a force barrier producing luminous radiation through fluorescence or excitation...

While I don't know whether the Freemasons and their cohorts ever really contacted the sort of beings who we would now term "extraterrestrials," it may be that they did. Or it may only be that they only thought they did. Certain areas of human history—and the history of disinformation—elude easy answers. Yet I can't help reflecting on the fact that contact with extraterrestrial aliens might have been just as profitable a pursuit then for the occult adept—and the rank charlatan—as it is today.

11

Occult Espionage

Elizabethan scholar Francis Yates places John Dee, Illuminatus Extraordinaire, at the center of the formation of the Rosicrucian secret fraternity, this because of the references to *Ros Crus*, or the "Dew of Light" in his work. The Dew of Light is also a cabalistic image. Today we primarily know Dee as cabalist, alchemist, court astrologer to Queen Elizabeth, and ET channeler—at least one of whom who bore a close resemblance to a grey alien.

But Dee had another interesting side to his character that falls into the grey area between scholarly disciplines that few are willing to talk about. John Dee was one of the founders of what has come to be known as British Intelligence, which in its early days used alchemical ciphers of Dee's invention for passing secret messages. For what it is worth, Dee's code name was 007. As late as World War II, Himmler claimed that the Rosicrucians were a branch of British Intelligence, although my sense is that he may have gotten it backwards.

To this day, British Intelligence remains heavily Freemasonic in its membership. Peter Wright, the former assistant director of British M15, describes in his book *Spy Catcher* his initial vetting for a high-level position in the organization:

"Just wanted to have a chat—a few personal details, that

sort of thing," he [John Marriott, M15's personnel director at the time] said, giving me a distinctive Masonic handshake. I realized then why my father, who was also a Mason, had obliquely raised joining the brotherhood when I first discussed with him working for M15 full-time.

I'm reminded of an odd instance when a journalist friend of mine was covering a survivalist/patriot convention for an American magazine. During the course of the convention, he met Bo Gritz, the right wing Liberty Lobby's Populist Party candidate for president of the U.S. in 1992, Vietnam war hero, and a prominent personality in the patriot movement. Shaking Gritz's hand, he says that that he was rather surprised that he was given what he took to be a secret Masonic grip, and that Gritz looked at him in a somewhat sheepish fashion when he didn't return the grip. An interesting confluence of forces in play in the world these days...

Linking the Mother Goddess cult (of which Freemasonry is the most prevalent example that we know of) to intelligence agencies, the authors of *Dope, Inc.* give a highly interesting interpretation:

> The Cult of Isis was developed in ancient Egypt no later than the Third Dynasty of the Old Kingdom, approximately 2780 B.C. and represents one of the earliest formal articulations of the entropic and backward ideology of mother-worship. As known to the priesthood of the Temple of Isis—true believers themselves—the Isis cult formalizes the elements of a capability for social control, exploitation, and destruction of creative free will in subject populations. The elements include:
>
> Use of various schizophrenia-inducing drugs;
>
> Use of repetitive, heteronomic sounds in "music" to supplement the effect of psychotropic drugs, and to create a societal aesthetic that endorses and encourages the use of the drugs;
>
> Creation of synthetic cults based on the original reactionary Isis myth but specific to the psychological profile

of the population which the priesthood has targeted for subversion;

Enforcement of a political-economic model antagonistic to general human progress, and containing targeted populations within noncreative, manual slave-labor projects such as pyramid building. This combination of Pharaonic cult capabilities was taken as a model for further refinement in this century by the British Secret Intelligence Service's Tavistock Institute in London—an institution which launched the "counterculture" in the United States and Europe, based on the very drugs, mescaline and hashish, the ancient priesthood had employed.

The occult underpinnings of the spy business should not be glossed over if we are attempting to understand historical world manipulation by secret societies, much less the real nature of UFO abductions. It may be interesting to note that many occultists channeling "alien" entities have had one foot in the occult camp, the other foot among spy agency contacts.

Aleister Crowley was a "magickal" adept who functioned as a spy for the British, and—opinions differ—perhaps simultaneously for the Germans. During his career as the world's foremost occultist of the time, Crowley claimed to be in contact with any number of alien beings, including gods of ancient Egypt, and to channel written material such as *The Book of the Law*, which he attributed to an extraterrestrial entity named Aiwass. As noted earlier in this text, he also claimed he had contacted an alien named Lam, which, from the drawing that Crowley made of the entity, looks almost exactly like the big-headed aliens so often involved in UFO abductions.

A 1923 U.S. military intelligence report reveals that Aleister Crowley, as well as another famous occultist, Rudolph Steiner, the founder of the Blavatsky-esque Anthroposophy, were being investigated as the leaders of a New York occult group allegedly involved in "subversive Bolshevik activities." The report, written by a Norman Armond, goes so far as to suggest that the Russian Revolution may have been controlled by occult networks. Armond states that Steiner and Crowley, through a holding company Steiner controlled, had been involved in an alliance with Lenin that had begun in 1909.

Aleister Crowley is reported—whether reliably or not, I do not know—to have initiated "psychedelic guru" Aldous Huxley into drugs. While this connection may lie somewhat afield of what we are discussing, Huxley was the grandson of Thomas Huxley, a founder of the Rhodes Round Table, which was the base from which later well-known elitist control mechanisms such as the Trilateral Commission, the Council on Foreign Relations, and the Bilderbergers were launched.

Aldous Huxley was raised in the "Children of the Sun" (note the Sun orientation), a school for children of Round Tablers, and was tutored at Oxford by H.G. Wells who, during World War I, was the director of British foreign intelligence, and as the author of books like *The Open Conspiracy: Blue Prints for a World Revolution*, the most influential mouthpiece of the Rhodes/Illuminist New World Order.

During 1952 and 1953 secret meetings are reported to have taken place between CIA Director Allen Dulles, Ford Foundation Director Robert Hutchins, and Dr. Humphrey Osmond, Huxley's friend and personal physician. These meetings involved the funding by the Ford Foundation for a number of experimental research projects using LSD and mescaline. Also of interest is the statement of Captain Al Hubbard that LSD had been discovered, years prior to the date of its reported discovery, by a group led by the aforementioned Rudolph Steiner, seeking to discover a metaphysical "Peace Pill."

Huxley started a number of groups that, by furnishing LSD, mescaline, and settings for controlled trips, launched virtually all of the acid-occult missionaries of the 1960s, including Tim Leary, Ken Kesey, Richard Alpert (Baba Ram Dass), Gregory Bateson, and Alan Watts.

As poisonous as it may seem to a mostly-liberal audience, the LSD invasion of the world may have been a form of chemical warfare launched by British Intelligence (and their apparent masters), much in reflection of the kind of drug warfare that England had waged in the previous century during the Chinese Opium War. Certainly LSD and a connected doctrine of occultism as furnished by men like Crowley and Huxley has paved the way for future interventions of the occult (and possibly ufological) kind, and for a possible alchemical transformation of which we are only beginning to be aware.

The espionage strategy of drug and occult philosophy-induced destruction of a culture is reminiscent of the process that Carl Raschke attributes to UFOs in "Ultraterrestrial Agents of Cultural Deconstruction" in *Cyber-biological Studies of the Imaginal Component in the UFO Contact Experience*. Raschke believes:

> UFOs serve as facilitators of what I label "cultural deconstruction,"... "Deconstruction" is contrasted with "destruction" inasmuch as the latter connotes a random and unconstrained act of demolition, whereas the former suggests an aim-governed and formative sequence of changes... The work of deconstruction is not sudden, but slow and inexorable. It is more akin to a sculptor chipping away at stone so that he can craft a figure than to an iconoclast who seeks by some *coup de main* to obliterate outworn impressions. So far as UFOs are concerned, the deconstructive movement works upon human culture as a whole, although it may also have devastating effects at times on individual lives.

Another "child of Crowley" was rocket scientist, Caltech founder, and California OTO head Jack Parsons. In Pasadena, California in January of 1946, Parsons, assisted by Church of Scientology founder L. Ron Hubbard (who later claimed he was working in Naval Intelligence at the time) participated in a "magickal" working intended to incarnate the demonic Whore of Babylon via Crowleyan sex rites. At about the same time that Parsons was trying to incarnate an extraterrestrial entity, he also claimed that he had met a Venusian in the desert of New

Mexico—an interesting foreshadowing of the claims of later "contactees" such as George Adamski in the early 1950s.

Hubbard was later to abscond with Parson's girlfriend and his money, going on to form the Church of Scientology with its Freemasonry-like "grade chart" of spiritual processing and its cross emblem that is almost a duplicate of Crowley's *Book of Thoth* cross. Hubbard's son, Ron DeWolfe, says that Hubbard was something of an acolyte of Crowley, and after the death of the Beast 666, determined to take on his mantle.

Parsons was to die in June, 1952, in a chemical explosion that has often been suggested to have been a by-product of his cosmic tampering. That may or may not have been so. Before his death Parsons was interviewed by FBI agents and admitted that he had been illegally in possession of a number of classified documents relating to explosives taken from Hughes Aircraft Corporation, and that he had furnished them to the Israeli government. The question remains open as to who was responsible for Parson's death - infernal forces or Howard Hughes playing turnabout?

James Shelby Downard, in "The Call to Chaos" in *Apocalypse Culture* provides additional deep background on the intelligence agency-occult connection:

> Consider that the secret society which became the nucleus of the Office of Strategic Services - Central Intelligence Agency octopus was making biotelemetry implants in unsuspecting people as early as 1933. After the operations, the victims were kept drugged for a time and then were brainwashed (OSS-CIA is written that way because when the former became the latter, they changed the name but not the facts). I believe the implants were at first activated by touching the skin with a device similar to an electronic prod, but which actually was a symbolical phallus.
>
> The early implants were made to stimulate the pudenda nerve, when triggered, so that the sexually excited and amnesiac-drugged victims could be used in the sex circuses of the OSS-CIA secret order. Those victims were not

infrequently operated on while anesthetized by morphine and scopolomine, which produce analgesia and amnesia (twilight sleep, to esotericists). They too were brainwashed after healing. This evil program, supposedly for the sake of national security, was oriented to the Cult of GAOTU [The Freemasonic god, the Great Architect of the Universe].

Downard also reports:

Saturnalian orgies were and are performed with some representation of a deity... A woman I call the Great Whore performed in those rites some years ago, representing such deities as Artemis (Diana or Hecate), Aphrodite Porne (Dirty Venus), Bastet, Selket and the White Goddess described by Robert Graves in his famous book. I do believe that these sex circuses were part of a greater Call to Chaos working...

Is Mr. Downard projecting all of this? I am not entirely certain, but I do know that there are strong verifiable linkages between occultism, politics, and spycraft. One of the less-spoken-of aspects is their connection to homosexual and bisexual practices, long a mainstay of certain forms of ritual magick. With the risk of straying into Political Incorrectness (truth, as always, being a secondary concern of the arbiters of our national mindset), I will speak of such matters.

Jim Brandon in his excellent *The Rebirth of Pan* has commented on the attraction of UFOs, inexplicable Fortean events, and alien entities to sex activities of various sorts. It should be noted that homosexual orgies seem to have been an integral part of many Mystery Religion rituals, the precursor of many current secret societal practices, and that in primitive tribes homosexuals were often looked upon as partaking of divinity, and took on the role of shamans (read "channelers" in latter-day parlance). The Mystery Religions in addition utilized hallucinogenic drugs, Sun and Mother Goddess worship and human sacrifice—at least on occasion.

Aleister Crowley engaged in bisexual practices for some of

his magickal workings, as did the cabal of "Apostles," a Cambridge University student group that was thoroughly infiltrated by the KGB and took over British intelligence in the 1930s, their influence said to have continued until the present day. One of the founders of the Apostles, which was termed by members as "the Higher Sodomy" and "a sort of gay Freemasonry," was Sidney Reilly, "Ace of Spies" as the media has it. Reilly was also part of the Rhodes Round Table group at 120 Broadway in New York that provided funding for the Bolshevik revolution. An index to Reilly's viewpoint is provided in a letter on bolshevism that he penned in 1925:

> I believe that... it [bolshevism] is bound by a process of evolution to conquer the world, as Christianity and the ideas of the French Revolution have done before it... and that nothing—least of all violent reactionary forces—can stem its ever-rising tide... the much decried and so little understood "Soviets" which are the outward expression of bolshevism as applied to practical government, are the nearest approach I know of, to a real democracy based upon true social justice and that they may be destined to lead the world to the highest ideal of statesmanship—Internationalism.

Pretty straight Round Table-One Worldism in Bolshevik guise.

From the ranks of the Apostles came such highly-placed British intelligence turncoats as Anthony Blunt, Donald Maclean, Kim Philby, and Guy Burgess. These men were KGB agents who infiltrated and controlled the highest levels of British—and in certain instances—American spycraft. In recent years Victor (Lord) Rothschild of the Rothschild banking family (which bankrolled Cecil Rhodes), a member of British intelligence during World War II, was fingered in the British Parliament as the most likely candidate for the highly-placed "Fifth Man" Soviet spy among his Apostle friends Blunt, Burgess, Philby, and Maclean. Although there were calls for prosecution,

Margaret Thatcher defended Rothschild and within months the case was closed. The behind-the-scenes manipulation continues. Another homosexual cabal that allegedly included Knight of Malta, British intelligence agent, and Rhodes Round Table lawyer Louis Bloomfield, along with homosexuals Clay Shaw and David Ferrie, as described by "Torbitt" in his pivotal investigative document *Nomenclature of an Assassination Cabal,* is said to have been responsible—in an organizational sense—for the John F. Kennedy assassination.

There is a tangled web of Masonic symbolism that can be discerned in the events of the JFK assassination, beginning with the fact that the killing took place in the "Lone Star" (i.e. pentagram, Sirius) state. Remarkable research in this regard has been done by James Shelby Downard, demonstrating that the Kennedy assassination was manipulated for ritual purposes in an enactment of the ages-old "Killing of the King" fertility ritual, admittedly a radical theory but one backed up by a good deal of evidence.

As John Michell has said in *The Flying Saucer Vision*, "what we now suspect was in the past openly known. The 'gods' demand sacrifices, perfect specimens for their own scientific purposes. In the days when the nature of the gods was known, their desires studied, and the benefits they could bring enjoyed, sacrifices were left for them on the high places which they frequented. The relationship between the gods of mythology and the superior race from the sky, to whom the first sacrifices were made is a large subject which must soon be studied in detail."

In "The Call to Chaos" in *Apocalypse Culture*, Downard explains, "The third degree of 'Blue' (basic) Freemasonry, and more particularly the ninth degree of Scottish Rite work, embody symbolical assassination and death ritual; but in GAOTU [the Great Architect of the Universe] operations they go in for the real McCoy: heavy snuff stuff."

The Kennedy assassination was performed at Dealey Plaza, the location of the first Masonic temple in Dallas. "Security" for the Kennedy motorcade was supplied by the New Orleans CIA office, with headquarters in a Masonic temple building. Dealey Plaza is located near the Trinity River, and Kennedy's motorcade headed for the Triple Underpass, both references symbolic of the Masonic triangle and number three fixation. In what may have been a symbolic dramatization of the Masonic Hiram Abif legend of assassination by three "unworthy craftsmen," after the Kennedy murder three "hoboes" were paraded in front of cameras by the Dallas police (one of the "hoboes" alleged to be E. Howard Hunt of the CIA), then the three were quickly released without record of their identity. In Masonic lore assassins travel in threes.

"Torbitt's" investigations persuasively show that the conspiracy to murder JFK was run from the top by Masonic Vice President Lyndon Johnson and 33rd degree Mason and homosexual J. Edgar Hoover, at the time playing dual roles in Washington as Director of the FBI and epically repulsive party girl, with Bloomfield (also very likely a Mason because of his affiliation with British intelligence) running a large network of conspirators and underlings in the killing of Kennedy. Mason Lyndon B. Johnson appointed Mason Earl Warren to head the Warren Commission for investigation of the assassination. Information was doled out to the commission by Mason Hoover and Mason and ex-CIA director Allen Dulles, while 33rd degree Mason Gerald Ford seems to have done everything he could to discount the possibility that the murder had been perpetrated by anyone but a "lone nut assassin."

One macabre possibility is that Lee Harvey Oswald may have received the same sort of brain implant as the alleged saucer abductees mentioned earlier. As detailed in *The Man Who Knew Too Much* by Dick Russell, the Mexico City CIA station was, immediately prior to the Kennedy assassination, the location of certain mind control experiments intended to create a "sleeper killer," that is, an hypnotically-controlled assassin. Russell also repeats a "deadly rumor" that was published in the little-known

Were We Controlled? by the pseudonymous "Lincoln Lawrence." Russell reports:

Lawrence began his chronicle on March 30, 1961, when Oswald was admitted to the Third Clinical Hospital's Ear, Nose, and Throat division in Minsk [Russia]. He had been suffering "complaints about suppuration from the right ear and weakened in hearing," and the diagnosis called for an adenoid operation. Marina, whom he had recently met, came regularly to his bedside during his eleven-day stay in the hospital.

"After he was placed under anesthesia," Lawrence wrote, "advanced technique was employed to implant a miniaturized radio receiver which would produce muscular reaction in his cerebral region." Thus, upon leaving the hospital, Oswald would "remain for the rest of his life—without his knowledge—a completely efficient human tool... subject to control!"

The author went on to describe two devices implanted in Oswald's brain. One was R.H.I.C. (Radio-Hypnotic Intracerebral Control), "the ultra-sophisticated application of post-hypnotic suggestion triggered at will by radio transmission. It is a recurring hypnotic state, re-induced automatically at intervals by the same radio control"... On record in the National Archives is a government memo dated March 3, 1964, from CIA director McCone to Secret Service chief James Rowley, which makes a remarkably similar speculation. Following his surgery at the Minsk hospital, McCone wrote, Oswald might have been "chemically or electronically 'controlled'... a sleeper agent. Subject spent 11 days hospitalized for a 'minor ailment' which should have required no more than three days hospitalization at best"... But "Lincoln Lawrence" did not see Oswald ultimately as a pawn of the Soviets. Rather, he wrote that Oswald was later "high-jacked," or "maneuvered into the orbit of another group which trained and prepared him for work in the future when they (the second group) might have need for his 'special qualifications.' The second group then asserted control of

Oswald upon his return to the United States in the summer of 1962..."

According to Lincoln Lawrence, Oswald was not the only manipulated cog in the wheel. Another was Jack Ruby, "placed under hypnosis... perhaps at a party or perhaps by some 'performer' who was pretending to offer a casual audition for the Carousel Club." The entertainer at Ruby's club the week of the assassination was, in fact, a hypnotist, William Crowe, whose stage name was Bill DeMar.

It is verifiable that Masons and their allied secret societies are hardwired into the control systems of government and intelligence agencies, comprising a level of unseen motive and hidden intention in agencies that have the power of life and death over the citizens of the United States and the world. They control the controllers, so to speak, and if there was a conspiracy and a cover-up in the John F. Kennedy assassination, then they were certainly in a position to accomplish them.

James Shelby Downard, again, has stated:

> But the ultimate purpose of that assassination was not political or economic but sorcerous; for the control of the dreaming mind and the marshaling of its forces is the omnipotent force in this entire scenario of lies, cruelty and degradation. Something died in the American people on November 22, 1963—call it idealism, innocence or the quest for moral excellence—it is this transformation of human beings which is the authentic reason and motive for the Kennedy murder.

And the transformation continues...

12

The Year of Light

The calendar of the Freemasons begins four thousand years prior to the Gregorian, at the time of a reported supernova that they commemorate as *Anno Lucis,* the Year of Light, and about the same time that a fantastic leap in civilization was accomplished in Sumeria and Egypt. Look at the cornerstone of any government building in your town and you will see that the Masonic date is included in the inscription, obvious proof that this dating is highly important to the Masons. But there were other, earlier commemorations to the supernova. Richard W. Noone, the author of a book titled *5/5/2000,* believes that the Great Pyramid at Giza was probably built as a monument to this striking astronomical event. He states:

> The Grand Gallery [of the pyramid], aimed like a giant telescope at a particular celestial body in the earth's southern sky—before its view of the heavens was blocked by the completion of the building—points to where radio astronomy has just pinpointed the supernova (or giant stellar explosion) nearest to our solar system... The Great Pyramid's Grand Gallery is focused at this particular spot in the earth's southern sky.

Noone recalls that Dr. Anthony Hewish, 1974 Nobel Prize winner, while tracking astronomical anomalies in the heavens, "demonstrated that... strange rhythmic pulses were radio emissions from a star that had collapsed or blown itself up in the earth's southern sky some time around 4000 B.C." At about the same time that Hewish's research was taking place, George Michanowsky, author of *The Once and Future Star*, was deciphering Sumerian tablets that caused him to come to the same conclusion. According to Noone's review of the events:

> The ancient Sumerian cuneiform table Michanowsky was deciphering described a giant star exploding within a triangle formed by the three stars Zeta Puppis, Gamma Velorum, and Lambda Velorum...
> Michanowsky continued deciphering the Sumerian star catalogue, containing observations going back for thousands of years. The remarkably accurate star catalogue now stated that the blazing star that had exploded within the triangle would again be seen by man in 6,000 years.

This means, interestingly enough, that the Sumerians set the date for the reappearance of the supernova in about the year 2000 A.D. Strong evidence, it seems to me, that the Freemasons probably see the turn of the next century as having a pivotal significance in their mythic history of the world. Taking into account what seem to be the secret purposes of the Freemasons and other allied secret societies, there are certainly many speculations that could be made about what the nature of that significance might entail.

If you are still in doubt that behind the whitebread facade of world politics there is an occult agenda, read the following quotes published in the *Rosicrucian Digest* in 1948, and drawn to my attention in *The Patriot Report* of February 1998. According to an article titled "Requisites of Peace":

—Nationalism is destined to become extinct.
—The dissolution of nationalism does not mean advocating an equal distribution of the world's goods among all peoples. It

does mean a pooling of resources and their common control by all the peoples for the whole of humanity.
—A one world is inevitable.
—If it does not come through an intelligent admission of the obsolescence of nationalism, then it will come through the most terrible war conceivable.
—Does all this seem to strike at the love of country? It will mean only the replacement of a limited love for a more expansive and expedient one - the love of the world.
—A unity of people, not of states, is required; if there is a merging of interests then there also must be a merging of political control - a central government.

The following quotes are from another article from the *Rosicrucian Digest* published in 1948, "War or Peace," penned by Gisbert Bossard:

—The eventual solution lies in a world federation... the world has progressed to the point of a United Nations.
—Unless certain deficiencies in the U.N. charter are eliminated, the United Nations organization cannot exercise effective world authority.
—Your help is needed in the final push for victory.
—The first Reform: Abolish the veto in matters of aggression.
—The second Reform: Control atomic energy and limit all other important weapons.
—The third Reform: Establish an effective but tyranny-proof world police force.
—Russia will achieve military equality with the U.S. through quota disarmament.
—The cooperation of Russia for the "One World" and a new and wonderful era for mankind is essential.

Aside from the dark catalog of covert manipulation that I have compiled in these pages, I will not delude you into thinking that I am certain that the Freemasons are planning on overthrowing the world system on or about the year 2000 A.D. I do not even know for certain whether this is the date planned for the final consolidation of governmental systems into the New World Order. All I know is that the twists and turns of history are covered with the bloody fingerprints of Freemasons and members of allied secret societies who have intervened at key moments to turn the flow of history in hitherto unanticipated directions, and that everything points to the year 2000 as being an epic culmination in the mythology of these secret groups.

The Masonic architects of the French and Russian revolutions; the Masonic assassins of Archduke Ferdinand who touched off the bloody conflagration of World War I; the Masons who seem to have been responsible for the Jack the Ripper murders performed to stave off a deadly crisis in the Masonically-controlled British government; the Masons who controlled the investigation of and may have been responsible for the murder of John F. Kennedy; the host of Masonic controllers who lurked behind the gothic machinations of the CIA MKULTRA mind control programs; and the continued direction of international politics by Masons and their occultist brethren like P-2—all this makes it seem that the occult portents can now be seen as forecasting another intervention by the cabal.

Key to the creation of the New World Order is the economic and political unification of Europe. According to Cornelia R. Ferreira, writing in a monograph titled "The New Age Movement":

> The formula of the "United States of Europe" and of the "Universal Republic" (to be formed by Europe's merger with other world blocs) was first proclaimed by the Illuminati in 1793; has long been the slogan of the French lodges; was adopted in the 1920s by the Theosophists; and was discussed in American-German Masonic circles after World War II. Unelected European Commission president Jacques Delors, demonstrating the importance of European unity (and the totalitarian nature of the future world government), has threatened national leaders who do not unequivocally endorse

it, hinting that Margaret Thatcher's opposition caused her downfall.

The attempted unification of Europe, directed (as revealed in *Holy Blood, Holy Grail,* by Baigent, Leigh, and Lincoln) by the Priory of Sion, a secret order that may in fact underpin, be connected to, or even be the Masonic order under a different name, may be a stage setting for something even more earthshaking than a united European state. At the same time that the European Commonwealth is being put in place piece by puzzle piece, there are additional and highly strange prefigurements coming into view, one of the most odd being the multiple-thousand sightings of Eye in the Triangle-configured UFOs seen in Belgium, the headquarters of the European Commonwealth, and, more recently, in Arizona, USA.

If one understands the claims made in *Holy Blood, Holy Grail* (and a study of Masonic texts such as Pike's *Morals and Dogma* or Hall's *The Secret Teachings of All Ages* will substantiate these claims), a person of the bloodline of King David, descended through Jesus and Mary Magdalene, is to be enthroned in a newly reconstructed Temple of Solomon in Jerusalem, ushering in the messianic New Age. This reenthronement of the Davidic line was apparently also the hidden mission of the Knights Templar, who are said to have been the group from which the Freemasons sprang in Scotland after the suppression of the Knights.

The family line from which the "Lion King" of the New World Order will arise may be the European royal von Hapsburgs, currently led by Otto Von Hapsburg, the son of the last empress of Austria, and a prominent member of the Bilderberger Society. The family crest of the von Hapsburgs is the double-headed eagle seen on Masonic regalia, and the family has been historically connected to the Illuminati in a number of ways. Maynard Solomon in his book *Beethoven* states that the composer's "Emperor Joseph Cantata," which characterizes Emperor Joseph von Hapsburg as a lightbringer and a foe of darkness, was commissioned by the Illuminati. The commemoration may have been based on the Emperor's legalization of Freemasonry in Austria.

Another scion of the family, Archduke Johann von Hapsburg, in the late 1800s provided a huge gift of cash to a parish priest named Father Sauniere, which sum he used to build a temple to Mary Magdalene in France's Renne-le-Chateau. Mary Magdalene, alleged to have borne a child by Jesus—remember? Sauniere was also connected to the Hermetic Brotherhood of Light and the Priory of Sion.

According to J.R. Church, the author of *Guardians of the Grail*, "The Hapsburg dynasty which ruled the Holy Roman Empire since the 19th century, is the direct lineage of the Merovingian bloodline. The Habsburgs are reputed to be the family of the Holy Grail offspring of Mary Magdalene."

At this time the most probable candidate for the position of World King is Hapsburg's son, Karl, who is now thirty-five years old. Karl Von Hapsburg was probably smirking when he said, "The time for the [Hapsburg] dynasty lies in some happier tomorrow when a new Europe... will undergo a time of resurrection."

The Freemasons have always seen themselves as "the manipulators," "the builders," hence the name. One of the secret meanings of the Eye and the Pyramid (which, check a U.S. dollar bill, lacks a capstone, or a culmination, suggesting that it is unfinished) is a portrayal of this intervention in history, the guiding of events in what is cabalistically termed *tikkun,* or the "perfecting" of the universe—through disinformation, murder, seemingly whatever it takes.

The Freemasons seem to take positive delight in the deception they employ. In *Jack the Ripper: The Final Solution*, which implicates the Freemasons in highly believable fashion for the Ripper murders, author Stephen Knight describes the mindset:

> Freemasons applaud violence, terror and crime providing it is carried out in a crafty manner. One section of the

[Masonic] notes says humor is all important and the most
appalling crimes may be committed under its cloak. The one
Ripper letter likely to have been genuine suggests that Jack
the Ripper was going about his crimes in just this way,
committing ghoulish murders with a Puckish sense of fun. If
Masonic supremacy appears in jeopardy, it is reestablished by
a show of strength, by crimes of violence, perpetrated to
demonstrate... the far reaching power of Freemasonry to
initiates the world over...

This is akin to the manipulation we are witnessing. Both
Christians and Jews will see the coming World King as the
fulfillment of their religious prophecies. What they will not see
is a cool precision of cogwheels in motion in the program that
enthrones him.

The date the Sumerians and apparently the Masons set for the
reappearance of the supernova within the triangle of Zeta
Puppis, Gamma Velorum, and Lambda Velorum is around the
year 6000 A.L. *(Anno Lucis)* or 2000 A.D.

Who knows? It may even be that the Masons believe their
own legends about Sirius, and expect the year 2000 to see the
return of the Oannes, the Nommo, the beings from Sirius, those
beings no doubt having plans for setting into motion another
stage in the civilizing of humanity.

A possible strategy to take advantage of this event is only too
obvious. If the Masons really are planning on setting a World
King on the throne—and they are—it would be to their advantage to take into consideration millennial beliefs widely held by
Christians about a Second Coming around the year 2000, while
at the same time taking advantage of Jewish expectations about
the Messiah and the rebuilding of the Temple of Solomon. They
have even been subliminally introducing the youth of the world
to the concept through the recent extremely popular animated
feature produced by Disney Studios: "The Lion King"—if you
doubt the explicit rendering of the messianic legend into huggy
and merchandisable animal format, then view this film another
time.

At the same time that we see the building blocks being pressed into place for the coronation of a World King, we see other curious activities taking place. Pulitzer Prize-winning investigative reporter Tim Weiner, in *Blank Check,* observes that the largest "black" or hidden budget expenditure by the U.S. military and FEMA (the Federal Emergency Management Agency) is in the creation of huge underground bases of the same sort that are mentioned in the wilder of the government-alien collaboration scenarios. Those scenarios of grey aliens ruling underground roosts and preparing for an invasion to be launched from underground, may in fact be disinformation masking what is really taking place: the elite in the government creating a safe underground haven for themselves when the Global 2000 plan goes into place.

The event which may prompt the placing of the key piece in the *Novus Ordo Seculorum* pyramid, the missing capstone, the culmination of the Fool's journey of the Tarot, may well be the catastrophic collapse of the U.S. economic system. The collapse of the U.S. currency and the stock market, as prefigured by the recent crises in the Orient, may well be the straws that will break the American Phoenix's back.

On the other hand, there are those who say that the widespread computer flaw termed the "Millenium Bug" or "Y2K" may perform the same function. The Congressional Research Service describes the problem this way:

> Most computer systems in use today record dates in a format using a two digit number for the year; for example, 96 represents the year 1996. The two digit year field is very common among older systems, designed when memory storage was more expensive, but is also used in many systems built today. With this format, however, the year 2000 is indistinguishable from 1900. The year data filed in computer programs performs various functions, such as calculating age, sorting information by date, or comparing multiple dates.

Thus, when years beyond 1999 are entered under this format, computer systems will fail to operate properly.

Here are some newspaper quotes about the possible effect of the Millenium Bug:

> For some institutions... it will be too late. We could end up with a real catastrophe that could affect many people's lives around the globe... One industry expert has called the defect "the most devastating Virus ever to infect the world's business and information technology systems."
>
> —*Washington Post*, September 15, 1996

> The [IRS] is launching a massive effort to forestall a breakdown of the income tax system when the year 2000 arrives... If the agency cannot quickly revise millions of lines of obscure software code... it will throw the government's financial operations into chaos. Computers throughout government and private industry face the same problem... Experts say the federal government has been dangerously late in recognizing the problem.
>
> —*Los Angeles Times*, October 16, 1996

> The world of finance... is especially vulnerable... The absolute worst case is a global financial meltdown. Clearing and settlement of transactions could break down. Stocks held electronically could be wiped out. Interest might not be properly credited. Deposits or trades might not be credited to an account. The consequences may be catastrophic.
>
> —*Business Week*, August 12, 1996

This book, however, is not a treatise on the Millenium Bug, and so I will not go into all of the possible ramifications of a majority of the computers in the world suddenly being rendered non-functional, but can you imagine the effects on this country—particularly in the inner city—if welfare and social security checks were not delivered for a few months?

Events of the sort mentioned above would leave the country, ripped apart by strife, ripe for elitist intervention. After push does come to shove, the small groups of survivalists and patriots hanging out in the woods of Oregon will provide little more than possibilities for further Establishment PR coups as these "murderous terrorists" are routed out.

There will be no resistance. Hungry, threatened people would be eager for any answer, especially if it was transmitted in "divine" fashion, and seemingly from the stars.

Regardless of whether there are any bigheaded grey aliens in the bleachers for the gala coronation, whether or not the occultists at the top are able to launch a fleet of UFO-style flying disks to perform synchronized aerobatics over the newly-rebuilt Temple in Jerusalem, wouldn't the appearance of a singularly impressive stellar display, a supernova flaring forth in the midst of a triangle composed of three stars, be a wonderfully impressive and awfully convenient harbinger of the Illuminati World King?

UFOs at the Edge of Reality

A lecture delivered in Atlanta, Georgia, November, 1995

What I intend to explore today are some of my thoughts and opinions about the nature of UFOs and aliens and reality, based upon an interest that goes back to about 1957. I'm going to focus on some material suggesting that UFOs and ETs walk a fine line between reality and thought (or awareness). This is not to suggest that this is an illusory experience, however. I don't believe that the UFO experience is illusory. I want to explore what you might call the edge of manifestation of this UFO phenomenon.

I'm not suggesting that UFOs and aliens are imaginary, nor will I pledge that they are always completely, materially, solidly "real." Actually, I think that their existence challenges the tightly-formulated definitions of reality and imagination, and points up the limitations of those definitions. It seems to me that UFOs sometimes happily cross these lines of demarcation, and defy the definitions. The way they do this gives us some clues to something else, to the nature of reality, what is really real and what is possible, in terms of the understanding and potential expansion of awareness.

Reality is an amorphous concept. My experience suggests that there is an in-between realm in this universe or omniverse where thought and matter meet, like one of those paradoxical graphics by the Dutch artist M.C. Escher, where thought and matter coalesce and partake of each other, where matter manifests from pure awareness, where reality takes form... and that the nurturing bed where matter, reality and, incidentally, where UFOs and ETs manifest, is what we might loosely call awareness, or the mind.

When I say "mind," I'm not limiting that to the purely physical conception, to the computer that resides behind your forehead, to the electrical activity sparking in your brain pan, or whatever, because that is a rather limited and limiting conception. If we stick with that, we're not going to accomplish what I want, which is to provide a little more familiarity with this borderland reality, with the interface between thought and material solidity.

When I use the term "mind" I am talking about awareness in a generalized sense, in a theoretically absolute sense. My own belief is that awareness is not necessarily limited to an awareness resident in the body, in a meat body. You can believe anything you want, but anyone who has any experience with meditation, with hallucinogens, or with ritual magic is going to have a sense of what I'm suggesting.

Awareness, as far as I am concerned, and in my own experience, ultimately has no limitations whatsoever, beyond the limitations that it conceives for itself. Awareness is potentially a creator, and it can create freedoms and it can create limitations. Awareness, interestingly enough, creates its own conception of itself, which is what it then proceeds to be.

I just want you to try on the concept that awareness may not proceed from solid reality. In fact, I'm not certain that I could prove this to you unless you were willing to entertain this possibility and play around with it a little bit yourself. If you think that the possibilities that I have mentioned are absolutely impossible, then you are maintaining that the beliefs and knowledge of this insignificant tide pool of awareness, the planet Earth, determine the possibilities of the entire universe. This has a corollary that UFO aficionados are often vocally decrying; the absurdity of people who believe that life could only exist on one planet in this vast universe.

I'm also saying that awareness, very loosely defined, is senior to solid matter. It stands above solid matter. Awareness creates thought and belief and, ultimately I think is the creator of solid matter. Reality, I believe is defined and created from this immaterial plane of thought and mind. I think that you create the entirety of your physical reference, and the only reason this isn't obvious to everyone is that one also creates the belief that one can't create or even influence physicality to the slightest degree with the mind.

I believe that you create your own reality entirely. In addition, you create yourself according to whatever template you choose, in whatever body you choose, on whatever planet you choose, based upon your belief structures.

It follows that if you create your own reality, if you change your beliefs about what you can and can't do, can and can't experience, can and can't see, then you can change your reality. You can restructure your own experience entirely, change your identity entirely, and experience anything whatsoever that you wish. This is perfectly true, at least in my own experience and belief structure.

Reality. The word is a semantic absurdity. Reality, according to my American Heritage dictionary, is "the quality or state of being actual or true." When you look up "actual" or "true" you find that defined as "Consistent with... reality." The definition goes in circles, and is never grounded in anything that is separate and verifiable.

The problem is that the concept of reality is indefinable, and the concept of something being "real" is dependent upon proving that something is "real," with a verifiable existence which is apart from some subjective belief or illusion. Something that can be nailed down using a disinterested measuring stick of comparison. Unfortunately or fortunately, so far as I know, it is impossible to do this with any aspect of reality or of thought. The reason for this can be exhibited by hauling forth the standard argument one encounters for the existence of something called "reality." I don't know how many times I've heard this one. You're talking to the guy at the party and presenting your crazy ideas about how reality isn't real, and the guy stands up and [bangs on the podium]. "See," he says, "This is real. This is solid. This is reality! Try and disprove that!"

The point is that knocking on something, feeling something, feeling the weight of something, does not prove its existence, because you are proving its existence with something that is essentially identical, that is, a solid hand is impacting with a solid podium. You have not removed yourself from the context of that existence and compared it with "reality."

It might as well be meaningless babble that takes place in a dream. You might as well be dreaming that you're banging your hand against a podium and hearing the rap in the dream. In fact, every time you do that, pound on the podium, you are dreaming in a sense, because solidity, solid reality, is not the basis of reality. You can dream that you're touching solidity, you can imagine it, and in fact, once you start working with this thing called imagination, once you regularly exercise your ability to dream up realities and all of the perceptions that are allied with them, you'll also be exercising your ability to mold and transform this one, that which you've considered to be your original reality. You'll theoretically be able to change your reality and everyone else's in any manner you wish. That might seem like a contradiction, but I don't think that it is: that you can change another person's reality. The reason it seems like a contradiction is that you are identifying your awareness with the limited definition of being fixated in a single physical body. You're really not stuck.

In my experience, there really is no "other" whose reality toes you're going to step on if you get a little too frisky with your awareness play, but it is one awareness inhabiting a multitude of bodies. At least until you change that conception, and that reality.

So the "truth" about "reality," bottom line, is that there ain't no such beast. Reality is only what we believe it to be. Reality is only a contingency of awareness. The fact that ten people or a thousand people believe the same thing, does not render the thing any more real in an absolute sense, but it does point out the structural underpinning of the determinant of this shared illusion called reality, what causes it to manifest in the shapes and forms that it does; and that determinant, that reality-shaper is called "belief." What people believe down deep is what they consider to be reality, and also what they experience. Sometimes this can be different from what they say they believe.

The existence of UFOs can be voted down due to the relative rarity of the experience, and its sometimes insubstantial character. It's the same thing with people who study conspiracy politics. You look into this subject and it becomes quite apparent that the world is run on conspiratorial lines, Rockefeller, Rothschilds, regardless of what Rush says. But the conspiracy is outvoted by the pundits in the media who know better without actually having researched the subject, and so it's not true, it's not real.

What can be accomplished by playing around with belief systems? I think that potentially we can remove finally all barriers to perception, to creation, and theoretically come up with an unlimited awareness, capable of knowing anything, capable of doing anything, and one which is totally free of limiting definition. This naturally smacks of conceptions of godhood, but I'm not trying to get religious here. I'm saying that this is part of the spectrum of possibilities of awareness. Human beings are part of the spectrum of possible awareness manifestations; snails are another.

And in this latter portion of the 20th Century mankind has come up to having awareness characteristics, enough smarts where it is possible to attain states of awareness that were hitherto unimagined, at least by the majority of awareness points on the planet. Of course, this is a belief structure in itself that I am communicating; that we are on this planet, that we are human life forms, that we have certain awareness characteristics, that we inhabit bodies, that there is such a thing as time and human evolution.

Awareness is a fascinating thing and in my belief, if consciousness that has been localized on the planet Earth would finally begin to flow a little and be liberated from some of its former boundaries and self conceptions. Awareness just won't stay in a localized, fixated condition and position forever. That's its nature.

The human condition is an interesting thing. I thought about just what the human condition is, what a human body is, what this fleshly container for our awareness is, and I think I've had some insight on this. It occurred to me that a real reality, something that you know is true, is more satisfying to awareness than simply a dream or a work of art or a movie, let's say.

It's far more interesting to an awareness to be involved in something that is real, something unchangeable, something that cannot be denied, a true story, let's say. And that's what the human body is all about. It is the awareness creating itself solidly inside of the drama, the awareness play making itself a solid portion of the play so that the drama is real!

The awareness of death even creates itself within the illusion that when the reality creation ends, when the structuralization ends, the awareness ceases to exist. This doesn't actually seem to be the case. But the solid creation of the human body—pinch me so that I know I'm not dreaming—is based upon interest. So long as you are an omniscient awareness that exists outside of its creation, knowingly having created or creating that reality or game or whatever, it's not half as interesting. You know that your creation is an illusion, it's a game, a movie, it's pretend.

You, the awareness, know that it is a form of play that you're experiencing and that it really doesn't ultimately matter. But to pretend that it's real, true, that it's reality, to put yourself in the 3-D holographic picture and say that you had no hand in its creation and that the physical creation in fact was responsible for creating you, that you were born into it and had no hand in the creation of the drama, now that makes for some real involvement, some real fun even if it's only of the tragicomic sort!

Ultimately, consciousness has to flow. It works like a rushing stream of events. No single, localized event ultimately has any meaning; only its localized meaning. It draws its meaning from the larger context. As we expand in terms of our own self conception, as we free ourselves from self-created barriers and limitations, you might say that we are refamiliarizing ourselves with the energy of the ocean of awareness, rather than fixating on the energy swirlings locked in the little tide pool, the tide pool of Homo Sapien's conception and delusion at the tail end of the 20th Century.

There seems to be a cover-up going on about the fact that awareness creates reality, is actually in charge of reality, and that awareness has the capability of creating a belief that something is solid and then perceiving it that way. Who's doing the cover-up? Well, scientists, I suppose, and the guys who don't believe in ESP and the paranormal, and of course if people believe this there wouldn't be any organized religion, so I guess the priests are covering this up, and maybe the societal structure, the elitists who don't want the commoners getting any delusions of grandeur that they can do anything they want and throw the bums out of the Federal Reserve or whatever...

There really is a reality monopolization going on and a continual indoctrination that is forever insisting on the limited nature of awareness. "I'm only human, it's human to err, you only go round once so grab all the gusto you can..." This is the tree of knowledge of good and evil that we're not supposed to pick from. Knowledge which, you might note, is proffered by the phallic serpent, Pandora's box (a cteic symbol), Tower of Babel (another phallic symbol), and the Frankenstein story where the moral is that you shouldn't muck about too much with reality because it's likely to bite you if you do.

The antidote to all this is the *Wizard of Oz,* written by the Freemason L. Frank Baum, where some upstart and her dog stop trembling for a moment and she gets up off her knees and sneaks away from the Scarecrow (Christianity, perhaps, with the crucified scarecrow?), the Tin Man (mechanistic science, perhaps?), and the Lion (animal impulses, perhaps), and Dorothy peers behind the emerald curtain (the green coloration perhaps signifying life, delving into the meaning behind this life). And then the deception becomes apparent.

Who, ultimately, is responsible for the cover-up of the centuries, the cover-up of the unlimited nature of consciousness? I would guess that it is awareness itself, the mass consciousness behind all of the mobile meat bodies, the mass consciousness itself which is covering up this possibility through its subservient minions like the priests and the scientists and the hack storytellers at NBC and so forth.

What would be the reason that mass consciousness, possibly the closest thing to God that we have pinpointed in this sector, has been covering up these cool abilities and transcendent possibilities? Possibly for fun. Possibly to create a game, because games have both freedoms and barriers resident in them, and this makes for interest because if you can do anything whatsoever then you create a completely non-challenging state. Superman, actually, would get pretty bored on Earth, because he wouldn't have any challenges. That's why the authors of the comic book had to invent Kryptonite, to give Superman a challenge with which to create a story.

Another reason for the enforcement of limited states and the cover-up of the real possibilities inherent in life is that there is a gradual unfoldment taking place in which this physical reality, bodies and so forth, is being evolved from non-existence or potential into a state of pure awareness. "God," let us say, taking part in a continual enlargement of its awareness and manifestation. Reality, I am coming to believe, is based solely and entirely upon the belief structures that awareness holds. Change the underlying beliefs and you will change the perception of reality.

One of the time-honored methods of reality manipulation and creation is ritual magic. Ritual magic, at least according to the more intellectual magicians that I have come across, is simply the channeling of attention through ritual and symbology, concentrating attention in a certain direction so as to achieve a certain result. The channeling of thought so as to create a certain physical manifestation. Basically the imagining of something purely conceptual into reality. Ritual magic as reality creation.

I don't mean to defame any ritual magicians who are in the audience, but it's obvious that engaging in magic is giving some of your power away. It's based upon belief in the limitation of your own power, and that you have to access some higher conception or entity or universe energy channeling device like a symbol, or whatever. You have to go through certain incantations and steps and buff your body with lambs wool, or whatever. It's based upon the belief that you need a servo-mechanism to channel a higher power in order to manifest whatever you want in this world.

More to the point, I would think, would be to locate the limiting belief you have about your own power and ability, to deconstruct that belief by realizing that you created it in the first place, and then to manifest directly whatever it is you want without employing a go-between. Cut out the Baphometic middle man.

It's interesting to note the interplay of the psyche with the techniques of ritual magic and religion. Both religion and magic, these techniques of creating or influencing reality, can be seen to derive at least in part from a hierarchical vision of reality, to contain trappings in their rituals and literature if only subconsciously dramatizing a subjection to kingly and noble forces. A totalitarianism of the spirit. In other words, I think that ritual magic and religion both have inherent in them the presumption of control by the nobility and a ministering court. If only in the hierarchies of angels. Or the *Wizard of Oz,* again. God as king, as above so below, regal robes, and the altar as the throne of the almighty. Jesus is coming - everybody look busy.

Actually, the study of reality creation and manipulation, in my opinion has been greatly furthered by the ritual magicians. In terms of the study of the creation and manipulation of realities, there is a succession of people who have contributed to this evolving field of study.

Certainly a lot of people contributed to this line of thought, but the most distilled transmission in this century, as far as I'm concerned, began this century with Aleister Crowley, who of course was also one of the first ET contactees with his channeling of the entity Lam. Several people have commented that Crowley's Lam bears a close resemblance to a grey alien. Was Crowley a black magician? Did he engage in human sacrifice? I frankly don't know for certain, but with his synthesis of Eastern and Western magical and religious thinking, you can see that Crowley knew that these systems are basically symbolic interpretations overlaid on and hopefully accessing something more amorphous, and that this, not the symbolism itself, is where the power derives from.

I'll put it another way: I get the impression that Crowley knew that all of this stuff comes from unmanifest, non- symbolized awareness, and that there is a stepping down that takes place from pure awareness by which symbols and realities are created.

The next guy in line in this transmission might be Jack Parsons, head of the Pasadena, California chapter of the Ordo Templi Orientis in the 1940s, who I think if he didn't teach L. Ron Hubbard everything he knew, then he at least quickened Hubbard's quest. Hubbard himself had lots of penetrating insights, although I would caution people about getting involved in his organization, which in my experience will siphon off all of your awareness and energy in the service of the Scientological cause. Hubbard also, although he came pretty close to copping to the fact that we create our own reality, also carefully hid that fact, because if you create your own reality you aren't quite so likely to subjugate yourself to "Source," which is what Hubbard termed himself.

Returning to the UFO/ET experience, from what I can tell, one of the things that makes it difficult to define and understand is that these are multifaceted phenomena, and there are a number of different origins for the experience. People assume that there is one explanation for UFOs/ETs, they latch on to the one they are most comfortable with, and they insist that one explanation explains all incidents and possibilities. I think that there are at least five different possible explanations for UFOs and ETs, in the following suggested categories:

(1) Encounters with aliens. People may have had encounters with extraterrestrial craft and their occupants, or with unexplained denizens of this world that seem to fit this definition; i.e. inner earth dwellers, or pixies or fairies, or whatever. Non-human encounters, let's say. This is an unproven possibility.

(2) Spiritual or non-material entities. This is the crossover dimension that I have been discussing, where reality slides in and out of thought and imagination and possibility and doesn't necessarily manifest as solidity or material reality.

(3) Government military operations involved with advanced craft and/or disinformation and/or psychological operations in which people are led to believe they have had encounters with aliens. I have the feeling that this is the source of some, although not all, of the more elaborate encounters over the last fifty years.

(4) The work of hoaxers.

(5) Misperception and delusion and fish stories.

So, depending on the incident, there are at least five possible evaluations and categories of experience. UFOs and ETs cannot be explained with only one explanation, and once you start compartmenting the experience this way, things become more understandable.

An example: As I recall, about two hundred years ago, the European scientific establishment declared that the panda bear was a myth. The rarity of encounters with panda bears made these men believe that the things didn't exist.

Now, can you imagine what the scene would have been like if the same forces had been at work on the "panda bear myth" as are at work in this century in relation to UFOs and ETs? Some guy in Leipzig would be running around in a fake panda suit, faking close encounters. The British military and the M15 intelligence agency would be doing advanced testing of fake, robotic pandas, and the CIA would be doing mind control experiments where guys were hypnotized and were convinced that they had a close encounter with a panda. The popular press would be full of this stuff. People would be dreaming of panda abductions. Disinformational panda manifestos and channelings from Panda Central at the center of the Earth or Saturn would be cranked out all over the place. We'd have faked panda autopsies. And the debunkers would be oh-so-seriously deriding the possibility that pandas could possibly exist. Like the UFO scene as it stands, things could get pretty confusing. Understanding the UFO experience has been confused by the propagation of hoax material, by the deluded and the true believers, and by the military trying to cover up its little schemes.

One proof of the unreality of reality is that so many totally unreal things that violate our conception of what is true continue to happen, regardless of how much government funding the materialists get. My own beliefs about UFOs and their inhabitants are perhaps influenced by two close encounters that I have had this lifetime, which I'd like to describe to you.

I was talking about some LSD experiences to a friend back in the late 1960s, and I said something to the effect that the hallucinations I had were incredible while under the influence of the drug. My friend responded, "They're not hallucinations." That struck me as a profound insight at the time, and still does. LSD and other hallucinogenics do not so much cause hallucinations as they cause a relaxing of one's barriers to experience and then the whole strange world rushes in.

By the way, I'm not recommending LSD or other drugs, I personally stopped this line of inquiry before 1970. But... the time of this anecdote is 1968, and I was tripping on mescaline in the San Bernardino Mountains outside of Los Angeles. I wandered off from the group of people I was with and climbed to the bed of a pristine canyon, and perched on a boulder amidst a trickling creek. I relaxed in order to ponder the fate of the universe. And that was when I saw Her, or perhaps just felt Her with complete perceptual clarity. She didn't have a body, but my sense was that the stones, the water, the trees, the air... these things were Her flesh. It was, maybe, The Mother, the Mother

Goddess who manifests this world... at least I thought so at the time. This may have been the same entity who has been worshipped since ancient times via such vehicles as the Mystery Religions, perhaps the same being as seen in Virgin Mary manifestations, Isis, Astarte, the White Goddess... but I was awe-stricken with the sudden realization of what was what, and an amazement that I could have ever forgotten that the world was the flesh of the Mother, my Mother.

And that was when she noticed that I was sitting there, and I thought I perceived surprise. She vanished out of there at warp speed, and I was left assuming—what could I assume?—that I was profane and undeserving of seeing Her and touching the hem of Her garment if she had been wearing one. Remember, she didn't have a body, but she was perfectly perceptible and understandable to me. So that was my first encounter with an uncommon being.

The second encounter was about four years later, in 1972. By this time I had knocked off the mescaline and LSD. Now, this was in the days before Whitley Streiber, and the media hadn't really latched on to grey aliens. But I woke up in the middle of the night in Los Angeles with one of these guys, the prototypical alien grey, staring me in the face, right up close. It terrified me, and I jumped out of bed and ran out of my bedroom into the living room. When I returned to the bedroom the visitor was gone.

I put this experience aside for twenty years, until I read the book *Communion,* which verified certain details of the experience, the primary one being the color and texture of the creature's skin... which was not grey, but blue grey, with the texture and reflective quality of clay... plasticine. That verification of detail was what made the needle swing over toward "close encounter" rather than "particularly vivid dream." I don't have those types of dreams. My nightmares don't feature aliens... and so now I am willing to accept that this might have been an actual encounter, one which may have taken place at the edge; at the edge of manifestation.

Regardless of the factuality or verifiability of these two encounters, I expect they did change my way of thinking about the UFO/alien phenomenon. These encounters violated all scientific laws and seemed instead to reside in something like a crossover state between fantasy and reality. Both of these entities simply vanished when confronted, and I began to feel that this might be the realm from which a good number of these encounters proceed.

A tangent that backs up this notion: it's interesting that a lot of ritual magicians have used sex as a tool for accessing different states of consciousness, for providing "oomph" to their workings. Although I'm not a member of the Ordo Templi Orientis group, I have a copy of their Gnostic mass, and it's a straight sexual symbolization, dramatization. Crowley was very much into this, Kenneth Grant, Austin Osman Spare, the Templars, the Mystery Religions, tantric yoga, even some of the Christian adepts like Baron von Zinzendorf's Christian-Freemasonic group who got their kicks from rhapsodizing about the ecstasy of using Christ's side wound as an orifice for their penetration.

Sex can provide an access port into energies that are useful in manifesting other realities... This, as in the case with drugs, may have something to do with the relaxing of inhibitions to experience. Sometimes, though, things are manifested that are not desired. In the Hebrew Talmud masturbation is warned against because with each act are created incubi or succubi or disembodied entities which they refer to as Qlippoth. Certainly it's no secret that in a lot of UFO abduction cases the aliens make free with the abductees, even going so far as having sex with them.

I also want you to note that researchers have long connected poltergeist, "noisy ghost" phenomena with the presence of pubescent children, children phasing into sexual maturity. Certainly a lot of energies are aroused during this period, energies which apparently manifest Qlippoth-like entities and even impact with the physical environment and toss dishes around and so forth.

I wonder if there's a correlation between alien abduction and sexual frustration? I know a woman who had an alien encounter and impregnation, or thought that this had happened to her, and she dramatized all of the signs of pregnancy, including the enlargement of her stomach. She's a New Ager so she wouldn't have appreciated my down-to-earth suggestion that she get a sonogram and find out what's really going on. Anyway, the aliens apparently intervened at the last moment and spirited the alien half-breed away before birth. I didn't question the woman closely enough to really have an informed opinion about what was going on—there are such things as what are termed hysterical pregnancies, and fathers sometimes dramatize the characteristics of pregnancy, you know—so I don't know the nature of what actually took place. But what I am pointing out is the sexual and birth connection to the UFO/ET experience.

Another matter of high curiosity is that ET abductions often contain elements which seem to be able to be traced to events which took place at the time of the abductee's birth. This was brought out by Alvin H. Lawson in a paper about what he calls the "Birth Memory Hypothesis." Lawson did a study of abductions in the 1970s and noted that in three hundred or so transcripts of persons who believed that they had been abducted by ufonauts, birth imagery was "abundant" in their descriptions of the events. These narratives linked "the fetus with the abductee, the placenta with the UFO, the cervical opening with UFO doorways... and the umbilical cord with levitating light beams or pillars..."

Lawson commented that "most" abduction accounts are "dominated" by prenatal details. I know this sounds speculative and pretty wild, but Lawson did additional studies in which he compared abduction sequences with events which actually took place during the person' birth, and noted striking correlations. For instance, in the case of one woman who had a breech birth (rear end exiting first), she got aboard the UFO "by being vacuumed up a tunnel, through a small door, and into a tiny bubble-like room (like the amniotic sac), where she remained throughout her experience. She exited the UFO in a unique manner..."

Remember, this woman was a breech birth. "She 'sat down' over a trap door in the floor and sank to the ground. Another subject, a breech birth, who was born feet first, exited the UFO by walking backwards until she was outside. A forceps-aided... breech birth, she said that 'they' pushed on her head, slipping her outside; later she said that during the examination 'they' moved her body to 'center' her."

Bud Hopkins says that he has regressed over 160 abductees whose narratives were loaded with reproductive imagery. Here the veil seems to have been pulled back a little, and we see the direct influence of the human psyche, at least in its sexual and birth aspects, directly influencing the UFO and ET experience, as if the psychic portion of the contactee is phasing into, shading into, shaping and influencing the reality of the contact, the actual circumstances. Might this be straight delusion? Sure, in many instances I'm certain that this is the case, but I don't think that we're talking delusion in all cases.

It's reminiscent of the anecdote where the shrink shows the woman a Rorschach test and she slaps him. I think it has more to do with the concept that Aldous Huxley talked about in *Doors of Perception,* that the mind functions, at least in part, as a reduction valve on experience, a tuner that limits the bandwidth of what is perceived, and puts perception into a manageable or understandable format, and perhaps even shapes the experience into what is dictated by the content of the awareness, particularly through its beliefs. I suggest that not only does awareness interpret what is perceived, UFOs and ETs and whatnot, but that it also creates these phenomena at both the mass consciousness and individual level.

Another suggestion that our experience of UFOs and ETs is influenced by our mindset is that a lot of these experiences portray far stranger motifs, ones which come from Freemasonry and the Mystery Religions and the New World Order.

The Frenchman Claude Vorilhon was taking a pleasant hike in the mountains one day, so he relates, when he saw a UFO hovering nearby, the craft bearing a Star of David with a swastika inside the emblem. A glowing childlike figure stepped forth from the craft. The child conversed with Vorhilon, bestowing a new name on him, Rael, and informed the man that the reason he had been chosen to be contacted was because France was the birthplace of earthly democracy (i.e. during the French Revolution). The being entrusted Vorhilon with the mission of building an embassy in which the aliens, which Vorilhon calls the Elohim from the biblical reference, could meet with dignitaries of Earth, with the stated purpose of spreading "Peace, Love, Fraternity."

Vorilhon was informed that humans had been created by the Elohim, godlike space travelers who were also skilled in the arts of DNA alteration and cloning. Vorilhon was now to assist the Elohim in preparing mankind for the final age of Revelation. Vorilhon, having adopted the name "Rael," now insists to his numerous followers that "a world government and a new monetary system must be created. A single language will serve to unify the planet." He and his followers sport the Star of David/swastika emblem that he observed on the side of the UFO, and they practice a form of "sensual meditation" which may be similar to tantric yoga as practiced by the OTO and other ritual magicians.

Quite obvious to anyone with a conspiratorial bent who has studied the literature are the New World Order/Illuminati references within this UFO encounter and the mission that was imparted to Rael. The childlike alien might as well have been on a mission from George Bush.

Another case is that of Betty Andreasson. Taking place in 1967, the events of Adreasson's abduction were later brought out through the use of hypnosis. Andreasson recalled being kidnapped from her home and spirited into what appeared to be a spacecraft. She was transported to an unknown location and then taken through a series of underground passageways that she believed to be part of a city.

Arriving at an underground chamber, Andreasson experienced, in a manner which she describes as highly painful as well as emotional, a kind of mythic psychodrama enacted before her that may or may not have been different from the kind of mystical dramatizations enacted in Mystery Religions and other mystic cults. She saw a huge bird, that she estimated be fifteen feet in height, which resembled an eagle but having a more elongated neck. The creature was apparently alive, but as Andreasson watched, it began to transform. It began to glow with a light and heat that was so intense it caused her pain.

When the heat and light vanished the bird was gone and she was gazing on flickering embers. As Andreasson stared at the embers she saw a worm wriggling in the ash.

"Now, looks like a worm," she described it in her hypnosis, "a big fat worm. It just looks like a big fat worm, a big grey worm just lying there."

Also during the experience, Andreasson was told by her abductors: "We are going to measure you for light... You have not completely understood the word that you have. You are not completely filled with light."

Andreasson said, "I believe that I'm filled with the light! I believe, I believe that I'm filled with the light!" Andreasson also recalled that, "They called my name, and repeated it again in a louder voice. I said, 'No, I don't understand what this is all about, why I'm even here.' And they, whatever it was, said that 'I have chosen you.'"

"'For what have you chosen me?'

"'I have chosen you to show the world.'

"Are you God?" Andreasson asked, "Are you the lord God?"

"I shall show you as your time goes by."

The following is part of an interview with Andreasson conducted by Raymond Fowler:

Fowler: Have they [the UFOs] anything to do with what we call the second coming of Christ?
Andreasson: They definitely do.
Fowler: When is this going to occur?
Andreasson: They know the Master is getting ready, and very close.

Since we are ranging cosmically far afield in our search for connections, it should be noted that Eye in the Triangle emblems have been seen on some UFO and the uniforms of their occupants, and that in recent years a significant percentage of two thousand UFO sighting reports in Belgium describe triangular craft with lights at each point of the triangle, and another light in the center of the triangle.

Anyway, the Lords of Light and various other references relating to light, the Star of David, the Phoenix, the Eye in the Triangle... All of these symbols convey a very earthly origin and are often seen in accounts of encounters and abductions. These are symbols from the mythology of the Freemasons and the Illuminati.

As I mentioned in my book *Saucers of the Illuminati,* incidents like these strongly suggest a Freemasonic/Mystery Religion/Illuminati motivation and/or manipulation. Both American and British intelligence agencies are still much aligned to Freemasonic goals, and so this might point out an intelligence agency connection, say in terms of staged incidents, mind control, whatever. That's the argument that I make in *Saucers of the Illuminati,* but since then I've come to see that there are other possible explanations.

There is the possibility that, since Freemasons and their ilk are quite involved in ritualism and magic, that this might be a straight magical transmission evoking these UFO events and even influencing them from a non-physical standpoint. These events may be summoned by Illuminati ritual.

At the very least I would suggest that these symbols might

have crept into the common subconscious coin, from which position they are dramatized in reality. Again, I am not suggesting that incidents like these are examples of delusion, but that we may be looking at something quite different: that the content of the mind can influence and shape the manifestation of real events.

Another clue suggesting the UFO experience draws part of its meaning from the human experience or the subconscious or mass consciousness experience is that one can see that one of the major concerns of this era is, and should be, the interface of human consciousness with outer space. We have finally evolved tools, that is rockets and other modes of propulsion, for travel among the planets, and are getting to the point where the creation of a faster than light drive is possible. We can see this as conceivable, and something that mankind may accomplish in the near future.

We might conceive that humans or mass consciousness may be pondering upon these things, upon this position in time and the possibilities inherent in it. And these experiences with spacelings may in part depend upon and be flavored by this focus of attention, but also possibly because we have not objectified our experience of outer space yet, we have not solidified our beliefs and views, standardized our interpretation of the possibilities of this experience.

UFOs may wholly or partly constitute an "imagining into" future possibilities. Perhaps a testing out of realities that we are going to put on or manifest in the future. A trial run in a new pair of shoes. Maybe like the Rorschach test, space is relatively amorphous to us at this moment, in our present perception, a somewhat neutral oracle that we are reading meanings into, that we are beginning to play with.

I suspect, although since I have not conducted the experiment I cannot prove, that there are major correlations between the type of UFO/ET encounters one has and one's chronic emotional tone... i.e. anger, apathy, grief, whatever; one's obsessions, philosophy, and material circumstances, roughly gauged.

I have the feeling that a statistical analysis would show significant correlations between people who feel that they are victimized and abused by life and those who feel that they are victimized and abused by ETs. I have the feeling that people who have a generally airy-fairy New Agey view of life might tend to encounter benevolent space brothers who impart homilies about transcendence and golden eternity. Naturally, this would not correlate on a one-to-one basis, it wouldn't always be true, but I think that a decent statistical sampling would show that I am on to something here.

Again, I am not saying that these non-human contacts with humans are not sometimes real. I am saying that we tend to attract experiences that correlate with our mind and emotional sets, and that we ultimately create our own reality, including traffic jams, bad television shows, toothaches, trips to the corner grocery, being a human on the planet Earth, and having our mind blown by an ET encounter. I think that we are God playing at being human, until we realize the fact and decide to consciously play at something different.

Another clue to the UFO/ET experience is the alien face. It seems to be an interpretation and distillation of information that is too overwhelming to comprehend, and so the perception is simplified into a context that can be understood.

I have the suspicion that at least in some instances the ET experience is so big, so amorphous, so alien, that it is simplified in its comprehension, into the grey alien face. And why might I think that? Because the prototypical grey alien face is based upon the least information units that you can interpret and still come up with a face. It can be reduced to three dots in an inverted triangular shape, and given that as the basis of a face, the details can logically be filled in to form a tiny chin and a big head. It works aesthetically, in the logic of the mind's eye. The triangular shape, the three dots in an inverted triangle, dictate the bulbous head as visual balance.

I am led to believe that perhaps the image is a distillation of an experience that is very amorphous but real, which offers a dearth of information—or perhaps too much information—to the contactee, and then the details are filled in by the mind. This is one function of the mind, to fill in the details. As a face, the grey alien is the ultimate in simplicity.

This is just conjecture, but is it possible that contactees and abductees in certain instances are confronted by something far more energy than entity, and that this energy field or nexus is channeled through the mind and interpreted based upon the least possible information units into the simplistic alien grey face?

You can see this in various oracular systems like the I Ching and the Tarot and runes and tea leaves and reading animal entrails and the Magic 8-Ball. These are purposeful destructurings of the field of information into random images, rendering the field itself amorphous and virtually meaningless, so that meaning can manifest, ready to deliver messages that are not otherwise available to the conscious mind. Like the William Burroughs Brion Gyson cut-up technique of literature. James Joyce must have seen this when he wrote his randomized *Finnegans Wake*...

John Lennon was pointing this out with his "I Am the Walrus" which is a randomized song text with recurring imagery of oneness and omniscient control by the Walrus, perhaps a bow to Lewis Carroll. This random fracturing of message is certainly the world of the abstract painter, like Jackson Pollock, and his swirling splatter canvases, which I find irresistible.

Ultimately I believe that there really is no universe, no "field" as it were, and no past and future. No time. I believe that we create the past to justify the present, and that we can create the past in any form we want. You create your own reality.

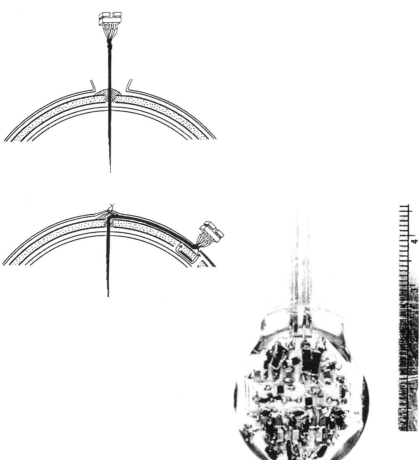

Implant technology pioneered by Dr. Jose Delgado.

Dr. Jolly West.

September 24, 1947.

MEMORANDUM FOR THE SECRETARY OF DEFENSE

Dear Secretary Forrestal:

As per our recent conversation on this matter, you are hereby authorized to proceed with all due speed and caution upon your undertaking. Hereafter this matter shall be referred to only as Operation Majestic Twelve.

It continues to be my feeling that any future considerations relative to the ultimate disposition of this matter should rest solely with the Office of the President following appropriate discussions with yourself, Dr. Bush and the Director of Central Intelligence.

Harry Truman

A White House document to Secretary of State James Forrestal on the creation of Majestic Twelve or MJ-12 dated September 24, 1947 and signed by President Harry Truman. Forrestal died mytsteriously on August 1, 1950 and was replaced on the Mj-12 commitee by General Walter B. Smith. From the German book *Die Dunkle Seite Des Mondes (The Dark Side of the Moon)* by Brad Harris (1996, Pandora Books, Germany).

Alleged photo from SS files of a Haunebu II in flight circa 1944. Note the Panzer tank canon mounted underneath the craft. From the German book *Die Dunkle Seite Des Mondes (The Dark Side of the Moon)* by Brad Harris (1996, Pandora Books, Germany).

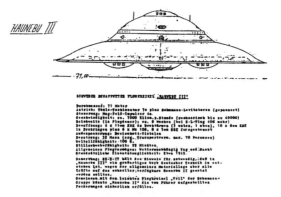

Alleged photocopy of SS plans for a Haunebu III being designed in 1945. From the German book *Die Dunkle Seite Des Mondes (The Dark Side of the Moon)* by Brad Harris (1996, Pandora Books, Germany).

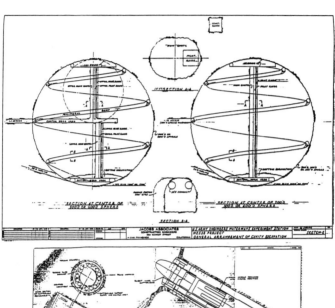

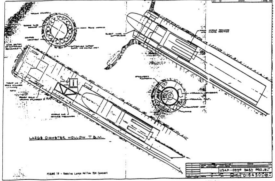

Above: Two methods of constucting a large, deep-underground cavity. Both utilize central shafts, a spiralling perimeter tunnel and work areas at the top and bottom of thea rea to be excavated. Excavation would proceed downward, starting at the top of the designated sphere. From the U.S. Army Corps of Engineers technical manual *Feasibility of Constructing Large Underground Cavities, Vol. III*. Below: An illustration from the U.S. Army Corps of Engineers technical manual *Tunnel Boring Machine Technology for a Deeply Based Missile System. Vol. I, Part 1*. Thanks to Richard Sauder and his book *Underground Bases and Tunnels: What Is the Government Trying To Hide?*

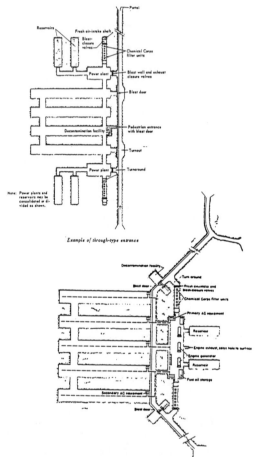

Examples of underground manufacturing and storage facilities from the U.S. Army Corps of Engineers technical manual *Design of Underground Installations in Rock: Protective Features and Utilities.* Thanks to Richard Sauder and his book *Underground Bases and Tunnels: What Is the Government Trying To Hide?*

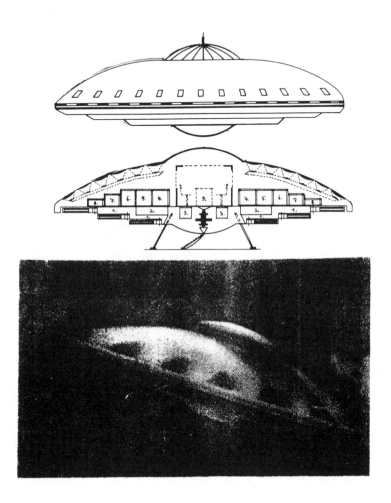

Jim Keith, 1949-1999.

CONSPIRACY & HISTORY

LIQUID CONSPIRACY
JFK, LSD, the CIA, Area 51 & UFOs
by George Piccard

Underground author George Piccard on the politics of LSD, mind control, and Kennedy's involvement with Area 51 and UFOs. Reveals JFK's LSD experiences with Mary Pinchot-Meyer. The plot thickens with an ever expanding web of CIA involvement, from underground bases with UFOs seen by JFK and Marilyn Monroe (among others) to a vaster conspiracy that affects every government agency from NASA to the Justice Department. This may have been the reason that Marilyn Monroe and actress-columnist Dorothy Kilgallen were both murdered. Focusing on the bizarre side of history, *Liquid Conspiracy* takes the reader on a psychedelic tour de force. This is your government on drugs!
264 PAGES. 6x9 PAPERBACK. ILLUSTRATED. $14.95. CODE: LIQC

INSIDE THE GEMSTONE FILE
Howard Hughes, Onassis & JFK
by Kenn Thomas & David Hatcher Childress

Steamshovel Press editor Thomas takes on the Gemstone File in this run-up and run-down of the most famous underground document ever circulated. Photocopied and distributed for over 20 years, the Gemstone File is the story of Bruce Roberts, the inventor of the synthetic ruby widely used in laser technology today, and his relationship with the Howard Hughes Company and ultimately with Aristotle Onassis, the Mafia, and the CIA. Hughes kidnapped and held a drugged-up prisoner for 10 years; Onassis and his role in the Kennedy Assassination; how the Mafia ran corporate America in the 1960s; the death of Onassis' son in the crash of a small private plane in Greece; Onassis as Ian Fleming's archvillain Ernst Stavro Blofeld; more.
320 PAGES. 6x9 PAPERBACK. ILLUSTRATED. $16.00. CODE: IGF

MASS CONTROL
Engineering Human Consciousness
by Jim Keith

Conspiracy expert Keith's final book on mind control, Project Monarch, and mass manipulation presents chilling evidence that we are indeed spinning a Matrix. Keith describes the New Man, where conception of reality is a dance of electronic images fired into his forebrain, a gossamer construction of his masters, designed so that he will not—under any circumstances—perceive the actual. His happiness is delivered to him through a tube or an electronic connection. His God lurks behind an electronic curtain; when the curtain is pulled away we find the CIA sorcerer, the media manipulatorÓ Chapters on the CIA, Tavistock, Jolly West and the Violence Center, Guerrilla Mindwar, Brice Taylor, other recent "victims," more.
256 PAGES. 6x9 PAPERBACK. ILLUSTRATED. INDEX. $16.95. CODE: MASC

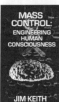

THE ARCH CONSPIRATOR
Essays and Actions
by Len Bracken

Veteran conspiracy author Len Bracken's witty essays and articles lead us down the dark corridors of conspiracy, politics, murder and mayhem. In 12 chapters Bracken takes us through a maze of interwoven tales from the Russian Okhrana with Costa Rican novelist Joaquin Gutierrez and his Psychogeographic Map into the Third Millennium. Other chapters in the book are A General Theory of Civil War; The New-Catiline Conspiracy for the Cancellation of Debt; Anti-Labor Day; 1997 with selected Aphorisms Against Work; Solar Economics; and more. Bracken's work has appeared in such pop-conspiracy publications as *Paranoia*, *Steamshovel Press* and the *Village Voice*. Len Bracken lives in Arlington, Virginia and haunts the back alleys of Washington D.C., keeping an eye on the predators who run our country.
256 PAGES. 6x9 PAPERBACK. ILLUSTRATED. BIBLIOGRAPHY. $14.95. CODE: ACON.

MIND CONTROL, WORLD CONTROL
by Jim Keith

Veteran author and investigator Jim Keith uncovers a surprising amount of information on the technology, experimentation and implementation of mind control. Various chapters in this shocking book are on early CIA experiments such as Project Artichoke and Project R.H.I.C.-EDOM, the methodology and technology of implants, mind control assassins and couriers, various famous Mind Control victims such as Sirhan Sirhan and Candy Jones. Also featured in this book are chapters on how mind control technology may be linked to some UFO activity and "UFO abductions."
256 PAGES. 6x9 PAPERBACK. ILLUSTRATED. FOOTNOTES. $14.95. CODE: MCWC

NASA, NAZIS & JFK:
The Torbitt Document & the JFK Assassination
introduction by Kenn Thomas

This book emphasizes the links between "Operation Paper Clip" Nazi scientists working for NASA, the assassination of JFK, and the secret Nevada air base Area 51. The Torbitt Document also talks about the roles played in the assassination by Division Five of the FBI, the Defense Industrial Security Command (DISC), the Las Vegas mob, and the shadow corporate entities Permindex and Centro-Mondiale Commerciale. The Torbitt Document claims that the same players planned the 1962 assassination attempt on Charles de Gaul, who ultimately pulled out of NATO because he traced the "Assassination Cabal" to Permindex in Switzerland and to NATO headquarters in Brussels. The Torbitt Document paints a dark picture of NASA, the military industrial complex, and the connections to Mercury, Nevada which headquarters the "secret space program."
258 PAGES. 5x8. PAPERBACK. ILLUSTRATED. $16.00. CODE: NNJ

MIND CONTROL, OSWALD & JFK:
Were We Controlled?
introduction by Kenn Thomas

Steamshovel Press editor Kenn Thomas examines the little-known book *Were We Controlled?*, first published in 1968. The book's author, the mysterious Lincoln Lawrence, maintained that Lee Harvey Oswald was a special agent who was a mind control subject, having received an implant in 1960 at a Russian hospital. Thomas examines the evidence for implant technology and the role it could have played in the Kennedy Assassination. Thomas also looks at the mind control aspects of the RFK assassination and details the history of implant technology. A growing number of people are interested in CIA experiments and its "Silent Weapons for Quiet Wars." Looks at the case that the reporter Damon Runyon, Jr. was murdered because of this book.
256 PAGES. 6x9 PAPERBACK. ILLUSTRATED. NOTES. $16.00. CODE: MCOJ

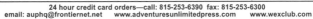

24 hour credit card orders—call: 815-253-6390 fax: 815-253-6300
email: auphq@frontiernet.net   www.adventuresunlimitedpress.com   www.wexclub.com

ANTI-GRAVITY

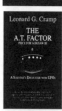

Leonard G. Cramp
THE A.T. FACTOR
PIECE FOR A JIGSAW III

A Scientist's Encounter with UFOs

THE A.T. FACTOR
A Scientists Encounter with UFOs: Piece For A Jigsaw Part 3
by Leonard Cramp

British aerospace engineer Cramp began much of the scientific anti-gravity and UFO propulsion analysis back in 1955 with his landmark book *Space, Gravity & the Flying Saucer* (out-of-print and rare). His next books (available from Adventures Unlimited) *UFOs & Anti-Gravity: Piece for a Jig-Saw* and *The Cosmic Matrix: Piece for a Jig-Saw Part 2* began Cramp's in depth look into gravity control, free-energy, and the interlocking web of energy that pervades the universe. In this final book, Cramp brings to a close his detailed and controversial study of UFOs and Anti-Gravity.
324 PAGES. 6x9 PAPERBACK. ILLUSTRATED. BIBLIOGRAPHY. INDEX. $16.95. CODE: ATF

COSMIC MATRIX
Piece for a Jig-Saw, Part Two
by Leonard G. Cramp

Cosmic Matrix is the long-awaited sequel to his 1966 book *UFOs & Anti-Gravity: Piece for a Jig-Saw*. Cramp has had a long history of examining UFO phenomena and has concluded that UFOs use the highest possible aeronautic science to move in the way they do. Cramp examines anti-gravity effects and theorizes that this super-science used by the craft—described in detail in the book—can lift mankind into a new level of technology, transportation and understanding of the universe. The book takes a close look at gravity control, time travel, and the interlocking web of energy between all planets in our solar system with Leonard's unique technical diagrams. A fantastic voyage into the present and future!
364 PAGES. 6x9 PAPERBACK. ILLUSTRATED. BIBLIOGRAPHY. $16.00. CODE: CMX

Leonard G. Cramp
THE COSMIC MATRIX
Piece For A Jig-Saw
Part 2

UFOS AND ANTI-GRAVITY
Piece For A Jig-Saw
by Leonard G. Cramp

Leonard G. Cramp's 1966 classic book on flying saucer propulsion and suppressed technology is a highly technical look at the UFO phenomena by a trained scientist. Cramp first introduces the idea of 'anti-gravity' and introduces us to the various theories of gravitation. He then examines the technology necessary to build a flying saucer and examines in great detail the technical aspects of such a craft. Cramp's book is a wealth of material and diagrams on flying saucers, anti-gravity, suppressed technology, G-fields and UFOs. Chapters include Crossroads of Aerodynamics, Aerodynamic Saucers, Limitations of Rocketry, Gravitation and the Ether, Gravitational Spaceships, G-Field Lift Effects, The Bi-Field Theory, VTOL and Hovercraft, Analysis of UFO photos, more.
388 PAGES. 6x9 PAPERBACK. ILLUSTRATED. $16.95. CODE: UAG

THE ENERGY GRID
HARMONIC 695
THE PULSE OF THE UNIVERSE

BRUCE L. CATHIE

THE ENERGY GRID
Harmonic 695, The Pulse of the Universe
by Captain Bruce Cathie.

This is the breakthrough book that explores the incredible potential of the Energy Grid and the Earth's Unified Field all around us. Cathie's first book, *Harmonic 33*, was published in 1968 when he was a commercial pilot in New Zealand. Since then, Captain Bruce Cathie has been the premier investigator into the amazing potential of the infinite energy that surrounds our planet every microsecond. Cathie investigates the Harmonics of Light and how the Energy Grid is created. In this amazing book are chapters on UFO Propulsion, Nikola Tesla, Unified Equations, the Mysterious Aerials, Pythagoras & the Grid, Nuclear Detonation and the Grid, Maps of the Ancients, an Australian Stonehenge examined, more.
255 PAGES. 6x9 TRADEPAPER. ILLUSTRATED. $15.95. CODE: TEG

THE BRIDGE TO INFINITY
Harmonic 371244
by Captain Bruce Cathie

Cathie has popularized the concept that the earth is crisscrossed by an electromagnetic grid system that can be used for anti-gravity, free energy, levitation and more. The book includes a new analysis of the harmonic nature of reality, acoustic levitation, pyramid power, harmonic receiver towers and UFO propulsion. It concludes that today's scientists have at their command a fantastic store of knowledge with which to advance the welfare of the human race.
204 PAGES. 6x9 TRADEPAPER. ILLUSTRATED. $14.95. CODE: BTF

THE BRIDGE TO INFINITY
HARMONIC

THE HARMONIC CONQUEST OF SPACE
by Captain Bruce Cathie

Chapters include: Mathematics of the World Grid; the Harmonics of Hiroshima and Nagasaki; Harmonic Transmission and Receiving; the Link Between Human Brain Waves; the Cavity Resonance between the Earth; the Ionosphere and Gravity; Edgar Cayce—the Harmonics of the Subconscious; Stonehenge; the Harmonics of the Moon; the Pyramids of Mars; Nikola Tesla's Electric Car; the Robert Adams Pulsed Electric Motor Generator; Harmonic Clues to the Unified Field; and more. Also included are tables showing the harmonic relations between the earth's magnetic field, the speed of light, and anti-gravity/gravity acceleration at different points on the earth's surface. New chapters in this edition on the giant stone spheres of Costa Rica, Atomic Tests and Volcanic Activity, and a chapter on Ayers Rock analysed with Stone Mountain, Georgia.
248 PAGES. 6x9. PAPERBACK. ILLUSTRATED. BIBLIOGRAPHY. $16.95. CODE: HCS

Man-Made UFOs
1944-1994
50 Years of Suppression

MAN-MADE UFOS 1944—1994
Fifty Years of Suppression
by Renato Vesco & David Hatcher Childress

A comprehensive look at the early "flying saucer" technology of Nazi Germany and the genesis of man-made UFOs. This book takes us from the work of captured German scientists to escaped battalions of Germans, secret communities in South America and Antarctica to todays state-of-the-art "Dreamland" flying machines. Heavily illustrated, this astonishing book blows the lid off the "government UFO conspiracy" and explains with technical diagrams the technology involved. Examined in detail are secret underground airfields and factories; German secret weapons; "suction" aircraft; the origin of NASA; gyroscopic stabilizers and engines; the secret Marconi aircraft factory in South America; and more. Introduction by W.A. Harbinson, author of the Dell novels *GENESIS* and *REVELATION*.
318 PAGES. 6x9 PAPERBACK. ILLUSTRATED. INDEX & FOOTNOTES. $18.95. CODE: MMU

24 hour credit card orders—call: 815-253-6390 fax: 815-253-6300

email: auphq@frontiernet.net   www.adventuresunlimitedpress.com   www.wexclub.com

ANTI-GRAVITY

THE FREE-ENERGY DEVICE HANDBOOK
A Compilation of Patents and Reports
by David Hatcher Childress

A large-format compilation of various patents, papers, descriptions and diagrams concerning free-energy devices and systems. *The Free-Energy Device Handbook* is a visual tool for experimenters and researchers into magnetic motors and other "overunity" devices. With chapters on the Adams Motor, the Hans Coler Generator, cold fusion, superconductors, "N" machines, space-energy generators, Nikola Tesla, T. Townsend Brown, and the latest in free-energy devices. Packed with photos, technical diagrams, patents and fascinating information, this book belongs on every science shelf. With energy and profit being a major political reason for fighting various wars, free-energy devices, if ever allowed to be mass distributed to consumers, could change the world! Get your copy now before the Department of Energy bans this book!
292 PAGES. 8x10 PAPERBACK. ILLUSTRATED. BIBLIOGRAPHY. $16.95. CODE: FEH

THE ANTI-GRAVITY HANDBOOK
edited by David Hatcher Childress, with Nikola Tesla, T.B. Paulicki,
Bruce Cathie, Albert Einstein and others

The new expanded compilation of material on Anti-Gravity, Free Energy, Flying Saucer Propulsion, UFOs, Suppressed Technology, NASA Cover-ups and more. Highly illustrated with patents, technical illustrations and photos. This revised and expanded edition has more material, including photos of Area 51, Nevada, the government's secret testing facility. This classic on weird science is back in a 90s format!
• How to build a flying saucer.
•Arthur C. Clarke on Anti-Gravity.
• Crystals and their role in levitation.
• Secret government research and development.
• Nikola Tesla on how anti-gravity airships could
  draw power from the atmosphere.
• Bruce Cathie's Anti-Gravity Equation.
• NASA, the Moon and Anti-Gravity.
253 PAGES. 7x10 PAPERBACK. BIBLIOGRAPHY/INDEX/APPENDIX. HIGHLY ILLUSTRATED. $16.95. CODE: AGH

ANTI-GRAVITY & THE WORLD GRID

Is the earth surrounded by an intricate electromagnetic grid network offering free energy? This compilation of material on ley lines and world power points contains chapters on the geography, mathematics, and light harmonics of the earth grid. Learn the purpose of ley lines and ancient megalithic structures located on the grid. Discover how the grid made the Philadelphia Experiment possible. Explore the Coral Castle and many other mysteries, including acoustic levitation, Tesla Shields and scalar wave weaponry. Browse through the section on anti-gravity patents, and research resources.
274 PAGES. 7x10 PAPERBACK. ILLUSTRATED. $14.95. CODE: AGW

ANTI-GRAVITY & THE UNIFIED FIELD
edited by David Hatcher Childress

Is Einstein's Unified Field Theory the answer to all of our energy problems? Explored in this compilation of material is how gravity, electricity and magnetism manifest from a unified field around us. Why artificial gravity is possible; secrets of UFO propulsion; free energy; Nikola Tesla and anti-gravity airships of the 20s and 30s; flying saucers as superconducting whirls of plasma; anti-mass generators; vortex propulsion; suppressed technology; government cover-ups; gravitational pulse drive; spacecraft & more.
240 PAGES. 7x10 PAPERBACK. ILLUSTRATED. $14.95. CODE: AGU

ETHER TECHNOLOGY
A Rational Approach to Gravity Control
by Rho Sigma

This classic book on anti-gravity and free energy is back in print and back in stock. Written by a well-known American scientist under the pseudonym of "Rho Sigma," this book delves into international efforts at gravity control and discoid craft propulsion. Before the Quantum Field, there was "Ether." This small, but informative book has chapters on John Searle and "Searle discs;" T. Townsend Brown and his work on anti-gravity and ethervortex turbines. Includes a forward by former NASA astronaut Edgar Mitchell.
108 PAGES. 6x9 PAPERBACK. ILLUSTRATED. $12.95. CODE: ETT

Tapping the Zero-Point Energy

TAPPING THE ZERO POINT ENERGY
Free Energy & Anti-Gravity in Today's Physics
by Moray B. King

King explains how free energy and anti-gravity are possible. The theories of the zero point energy maintain there are tremendous fluctuations of electrical field energy imbedded within the fabric of space. This book tells how, in the 1930s, inventor T. Henry Moray could produce a fifty kilowatt "free energy" machine; how an electrified plasma vortex creates anti-gravity; how the Pons/Fleischmann "cold fusion" experiment could produce tremendous heat without fusion; and how certain experiments might produce a gravitational anomaly.
190 PAGES. 5x8 PAPERBACK. ILLUSTRATED. $12.95. CODE: TAP

STRANGE SCIENCE

UNDERGROUND BASES & TUNNELS
What is the Government Trying to Hide?
by Richard Sauder, Ph.D.

Working from government documents and corporate records, Sauder has compiled an impressive book that digs below the surface of the military's super-secret underground! Go behind the scenes into little-known corners of the public record and discover how corporate America has worked hand-in-glove with the Pentagon for decades, dreaming about, planning, and actually constructing, secret underground bases. This book includes chapters on the locations of the bases, the tunneling technology, various military designs for underground bases, nuclear testing & underground bases, abductions, needles & implants, military involvement in "alien" cattle mutilations, more. 50 page photo & map insert.
201 PAGES. 6x9 PAPERBACK. ILLUSTRATED. $15.95. CODE: UGB

UNDERWATER & UNDERGROUND BASES
Surprising Facts the Government Does Not Want You to Know
by Richard Sauder

Dr. Richard Sauder's brand new book *Underwater and Underground Bases* is an explosive, eye-opening sequel to his best-selling, *Underground Bases and Tunnels: What is the Government Trying to Hide?* Dr. Sauder lays out the amazing evidence and government paper trail for the construction of huge, manned bases offshore, in mid-ocean, and deep beneath the sea floor! Bases big enough to secretly dock submarines! Official United States Navy documents, and other hard evidence, raise many questions about what really lies 20,000 leagues beneath the sea. Many UFOs have been seen coming and going from the world's oceans, seas and lakes, implying the existence of secret underwater bases. Hold on to your hats: Jules Verne may not have been so far from the truth, after all! Dr. Sauder also adds to his incredible database of underground bases onshore. New, breakthrough material reveals the existence of additional clandestine underground facilities as well as the surprising location of one of the CIA's own underground bases. Plus, new information on tunneling and cutting-edge, high speed rail magnetic-levitation (MagLev) technology. There are many rumors of secret, underground tunnels with MagLev trains hurtling through them. Is there truth behind the rumors? *Underwater and Underground Bases* carefully examines the evidence and comes to a thought provoking conclusion!
264 PAGES. 6x9 PAPERBACK. ILLUSTRATED. BIBLIOGRAPHY. INDEX. $16.95. CODE: UUB

KUNDALINI TALES
by Richard Sauder, Ph.D.

Underground Bases and Tunnels author Richard Sauder's second book on his personal experiences and provocative research into spontaneous spiritual awakening, out-of-body journeys, encounters with secretive governmental powers, daylight sightings of UFOs, and more. Sauder continues his studies of underground bases with new information on the occult underpinnings of the U.S. space program. The book also contains a breakthrough section that examines actual U.S. patents for devices that manipulate minds and thoughts from a remote distance. Included are chapters on the secret space program and a 130-page appendix of patents and schematic diagrams of secret technology and mind control devices.
296 PAGES. 7x10 PAPERBACK. ILLUSTRATED. BIBLIOGRAPHY. $14.95. CODE: KTAL

QUEST FOR ZERO-POINT ENERGY
Engineering Principles for "Free Energy"
by Moray B. King

King expands, with diagrams, on how free energy and anti-gravity are possible. The theories of zero point energy maintain there are tremendous fluctuations of electrical field energy embedded within the fabric of space. King explains the following topics: Tapping the Zero-Point Energy as an Energy Source; Fundamentals of a Zero-Point Energy Technology; Vacuum Energy Vortices; The Super Tube; Charge Clusters: The Basis of Zero-Point Energy Inventions; Vortex Filaments, Torsion Fields and the Zero-Point Energy; Transforming the Planet with a Zero-Point Energy Experiment; Dual Vortex Forms: The Key to a Large Zero-Point Energy Coherence. Packed with diagrams, patents and photos. With power shortages now a daily reality in many parts of the world, this book offers a fresh approach very rarely mentioned in the mainstream media.
224 PAGES. 6x9 PAPERBACK. ILLUSTRATED. $14.95. CODE: QZPE

HITLER'S FLYING SAUCERS
A Guide to German Flying Discs of the Second World War
by Henry Stevens

Learn why the Schriever-Habermohl project was actually two projects and read the written statement of a German test pilot who actually flew one of these saucers; about the Leduc engine, the key to Dr. Miethe's saucer designs; how U.S. government officials kept the truth about foo fighters hidden for almost sixty years and how they were finally forced to "come clean" about the foo fighter's German origin. Learn of the Peenemuende saucer project and how it was slated to "go atomic." Read the testimony of a German eyewitness who saw "magnetic discs." Read the U.S. government's own reports on German field propulsion saucers. Read how the post-war German KM-2 field propulsion "rocket" worked. Learn details of the work of Karl Schappeller and Viktor Schauberger. Learn how their ideas figure in the quest to build field propulsion flying discs. Find out what happened to this technology after the war. Find out how the Canadians got saucer technology directly from the SS. Find out about the surviving "Third Power" of former Nazis. Learn of the U.S. government's methods of UFO deception and how they used the German "Sonderbueroll" as the model for Project Blue Book.
388 PAGES. 6x9 PAPERBACK. ILLUSTRATED. INDEX. $18.95. CODE: HFS

THE TIME TRAVEL HANDBOOK
A Manual of Practical Teleportation & Time Travel
edited by David Hatcher Childress

In the tradition of *The Anti-Gravity Handbook* and *The Free-Energy Device Handbook*, science and UFO author David Hatcher Childress takes us into the weird world of time travel and teleportation. Not just a whacked-out look at science fiction, this book is an authoritative chronicling of real-life time travel experiments, teleportation devices and more. *The Time Travel Handbook* takes the reader beyond the government experiments and deep into the uncharted territory of early time travellers such as Nikola Tesla and Guglielmo Marconi and their alleged time travel experiments, as well as the Wilson Brothers of EMI and their connection to the Philadelphia Experiment—the U.S. Navy's forays into invisibility, time travel, and teleportation. Childress looks into the claims of time travelling individuals, and investigates the unusual claim that the pyramids on Mars were built in the future and sent back in time. A highly visual, large format book, with patents, photos and schematics. Be the first on your block to build your own time travel device!
316 PAGES. 7x10 PAPERBACK. ILLUSTRATED. $16.95. CODE: TTH

TESLA TECHNOLOGY

THE FANTASTIC INVENTIONS OF NIKOLA TESLA
Nikola Tesla with additional material by David Hatcher Childress

This book is a readable compendium of patents, diagrams, photos and explanations of the many incredible inventions of the originator of the modern era of electrification. In Tesla's own words are such topics as wireless transmission of power, death rays, and radio-controlled airships. In addition, rare material on German bases in Antarctica and South America, and a secret city built at a remote jungle site in South America by one of Tesla's students, Guglielmo Marconi. Marconi's secret group claims to have built flying saucers in the 1940s and to have gone to Mars in the early 1950s! Incredible photos of these Tesla craft are included. The Ancient Atlantean system of broadcasting energy through a grid system of obelisks and pyramids is discussed, and a fascinating concept comes out of one chapter: that Egyptian engineers had to wear protective metal head-shields while in these power plants, hence the Egyptian Pharoah's head covering as well as the Face on Mars!
•His plan to transmit free electricity into the atmosphere. •How electrical devices would work using only small antennas mounted on them. •Why unlimited power could be utilized anywhere on earth. •How radio and radar technology can be used as death-ray weapons in Star Wars. •Includes an appendix of Supreme Court documents on dismantling his free energy towers. •Tesla's Death Rays, Ozone generators, and more…
342 PAGES. 6X9 PAPERBACK. ILLUSTRATED. BIBLIOGRAPHY AND APPENDIX. $16.95. CODE: FINT

THE TESLA PAPERS
Nikola Tesla on Free Energy & Wireless Transmission of Power
by Nikola Tesla, edited by David Hatcher Childress

In the tradition of *The Fantastic Inventions of Nikola Tesla*, *The Anti-Gravity Handbook* and *The Free-Energy Device Handbook*, science and UFO author David Hatcher Childress takes us into the incredible world of Nikola Tesla and his amazing inventions. Tesla's rare article "The Problem of Increasing Human Energy with Special Reference to the Harnessing of the Sun's Energy" is included. This lengthy article was originally published in the June 1900 issue of *The Century Illustrated Monthly Magazine* and it was the outline for Tesla's master blueprint for the world. Tesla's fantastic vision of the future, including wireless power, anti-gravity, free energy and highly advanced solar power.
Also included are some of the papers, patents and material collected on Tesla at the Colorado Springs Tesla Symposiums, including papers on:
•The Secret History of Wireless Transmission •Tesla and the Magnifying Transmitter
•Design and Construction of a half-wave Tesla Coil •Electrostatics: A Key to Free Energy
•Progress in Zero-Point Energy Research •Electromagnetic Energy from Antennas to Atoms
•Tesla's Particle Beam Technology •Fundamental Excitatory Modes of the Earth-Ionosphere Cavity
325 PAGES. 8X10 PAPERBACK. ILLUSTRATED. $16.95. CODE: TTP

LOST SCIENCE
by Gerry Vassilatos

Secrets of Cold War Technology author Vassilatos on the remarkable lives, astounding discoveries, and incredible inventions of such famous people as Nikola Tesla, Dr. Royal Rife, T.T. Brown, and T. Henry Moray. Read about the aura research of Baron Karl von Reichenbach, the wireless technology of Antonio Meucci, the controlled fusion devices of Philo Farnsworth, the earth battery of Nathan Stubblefield, and more. What were the twisted intrigues which surrounded the often deliberate attempts to stop this technology? Vassilatos claims that we are living hundreds of years behind our intended level of technology and we must recapture this "lost science."
304 PAGES. 6X9 PAPERBACK. ILLUSTRATED. BIBLIOGRAPHY. $16.95. CODE: LOS

SECRETS OF COLD WAR TECHNOLOGY
Project HAARP and Beyond
by Gerry Vassilatos

Vassilatos reveals that "Death Ray" technology has been secretly researched and developed since the turn of the century. Included are chapters on such inventors and their devices as H.C. Vion, the developer of auroral energy receivers; Dr. Selim Lemstrom's pre-Tesla experiments; the early beam weapons of Grindell-Mathews, Ulivi, Turpain and others; John Hettenger and his early beam power systems. Learn about Project Argus, Project Teak and Project Orange; EMP experiments in the 60s; why the Air Force directed the construction of a huge Ionospheric "backscatter" telemetry system across the Pacific just after WWII; why Raytheon has collected every patent relevant to HAARP over the past few years; more.
250 PAGES. 6X9 PAPERBACK. ILLUSTRATED. $15.95. CODE: SCWT

HAARP
The Ultimate Weapon of the Conspiracy
by Jerry Smith

The HAARP project in Alaska is one of the most controversial projects ever undertaken by the U.S. Government. Jerry Smith gives us the history of the HAARP project and explains how works, in technically correct yet easy to understand language. At best, HAARP is science out-of-control; at worst, HAARP could be the most dangerous device ever created, a futuristic technology that is everything from super-beam weapon to world-wide mind control device. Topics include Over-the-Horizon Radar and HAARP, Mind Control, ELF and HAARP, The Telsa Connection, The Russian Woodpecker, GWEN & HAARP, Earth Penetrating Tomography, Weather Modification, Secret Science of the Conspiracy, more. Includes the complete 1987 Eastlund patent for his pulsed super-weapon that he claims was stolen by the HAARP Project.
256 PAGES. 6X9 PAPERBACK. ILLUSTRATED. $14.95. CODE: HARP

HARNESSING THE WHEELWORK OF NATURE
Tesla's Science of Energy
by Thomas Valone, Ph.D., P.E.

Chapters include: Tesla: Scientific Superman who Launched the Westinghouse Industrial Firm by John Shatlan; Nikola Tesla—Electricity's Hidden Genius, excerpt from The Search for Free Energy; Tesla's History at Niagara Falls; Non-Hertzian Waves: True Meaning of the Wireless Transmission of Power by Toby Grotz; On the Transmission of Electricity Without Wires by Nikola Tesla; Tesla's Magnifying Transmitter by Andrija Puharich; Tesla's Self-Sustaining Electrical Generator and the Ether by Oliver Nichelson; Self-Sustaining Non-Hertzian Longitudinal Waves by Dr. Robert Bass; Modification of Maxwell's Equations in Free Space; Scalar Electromagnetic Waves; Disclosures Concerning Tesla's Operation of an ELF Oscillator; A Study of Tesla's Advanced Concepts & Glossary of Tesla Technology Terms; Electric Weather Forces: Tesla's Vision by Charles Yost; The New Art of Projecting Concentrated Non-Dispersive Energy Through Natural Media; The Homopolar Generator: Tesla's Contribution by Thomas Valone; Tesla's Ionizer and Ozonator: Implications for Indoor Air Pollution by Thomas Valone; How Cosmic Forces Shape Our Destiny by Nikola Tesla; Tesla's Death Ray plus Selected Tesla Patents; more.
288 PAGES. 6X9 PAPERBACK. ILLUSTRATED. $16.95. CODE: HWWN

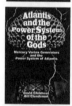
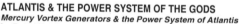

ANCIENT SCIENCE

THE LAND OF OSIRIS
An Introduction to Khemitology
by Stephen S. Mehler

Was there an advanced prehistoric civilization in ancient Egypt? Were they the people who built the great pyramids and carved the Great Sphinx? Did the pyramids serve as energy devices and not as tombs for kings? Independent Egyptologist Stephen S. Mehler has spent over 30 years researching the answers to these questions and believes the answers are yes! Mehler has uncovered an indigenous oral tradition that still exists in Egypt, and has been fortunate to have studied with a living master of this tradition, Abd'El Hakim Awyan. Mehler has also been given permission to present these teachings to the Western world, teachings that unfold a whole new understanding of ancient Egypt and have only been presented heretofore in fragments by other researchers. Chapters include: Egyptology and Its Paradigms; Khemitology—New Paradigms; Asgat Nefer—The Harmony of Water; Khemit and the Myth of Atlantis; The Extraterrestrial Question; 17 chapters in all.
272 PAGES. 6x9 PAPERBACK. ILLUSTRATED. COLOR SECTION. BIBLIOGRAPHY. $18.95. CODE: LOOS

A HITCHHIKER'S GUIDE TO ARMAGEDDON
by David Hatcher Childress

With wit and humor, popular Lost Cities author David Hatcher Childress takes us around the world and back in his trippy finalé to the Lost Cities series. He's off on an adventure in search of the apocalypse and end times. Childress hits the road from the fortress of Megiddo, the legendary citadel in northern Israel where Armageddon is prophesied to start. Hitchhiking around the world, Childress takes us from one adventure to another, to ancient cities in the deserts and the legends of worlds before our own. Childress muses on the rise and fall of civilizations, and the forces that have shaped mankind over the millennia, including wars, invasions and cataclysms. He discusses the ancient Armageddons of the past, and chronicles recent Middle East developments and their ominous undertones. In the meantime, he becomes a cargo cult god on a remote island off New Guinea, gets dragged into the Kennedy Assassination by one of the "conspirators," investigates a strange power operating out of the Altai Mountains of Mongolia, and discovers how the Knights Templar and their offshoots have driven the world toward an epic battle centered around Jerusalem and the Middle East.
320 PAGES. 6x9 PAPERBACK. ILLUSTRATED. BIBLIOGRAPHY. INDEX. $16.95. CODE: HGA

CLOAK OF THE ILLUMINATI
Secrets, Transformations, Crossing the Star Gate
by William Henry

Thousands of years ago the stargate technology of the gods was lost. Mayan Prophecy says it will return by 2012, along with our alignment with the center of our galaxy. In this book: Find examples of stargates and wormholes in the ancient world; Examine myths and scripture with hidden references to a stargate cloak worn by the Illuminati, including Mari, Nimrod, Elijah, and Jesus; See rare images of gods and goddesses wearing the Cloak of the illuminati; Learn about Saddam Hussein and the secret missing library of Jesus; Uncover the secret Roman-era eugenics experiments at the Temple of Hathor in Denderah, Egypt; Explore the duplicate of the Stargate Pillar of the Gods in the Illuminists' secret garden in Nashville, TN; Discover the secrets of manna, the food of the angels; Share the lost Peace Prayer posture of Osiris, Jesus and the Illuminati; more. Chapters include: Seven Stars Under Three Stars; The Long Walk; Squaring the Circle; The Mill of the Host; The Miracle Garment; The Fig; Nimrod: The Mighty Man; Nebuchadnezzar's Gate; The New Mighty Man; more.
238 PAGES. 6x9 PAPERBACK. ILLUSTRATED. BIBLIOGRAPHY. INDEX. $16.95. CODE: COIL

LEY LINE & EARTH ENERGIES
An Extraordinary Journey into the Earth's Natural Energy System
by David Cowan & Anne Silk

The mysterious standing stones, burial grounds and stone circles that lace Europe, the British Isles and other areas have intrigued scientists, writers, artists and travellers through the centuries. They pose so many questions: Why do some places feel special? How do ley lines work? How did our ancestors use Earth energy to map their sacred sites and burial grounds? How do ghosts and poltergeists interact with Earth energy? How can Earth spirals and black spots affect our health? This exploration shows how natural forces affect our behavior, how they can be used to enhance our health and well being, and ultimately, how they bring us closer to penetrating one of the deepest mysteries being explored. A fascinating and visual book about subtle Earth energies and how they affect us and the world around them.
368 PAGES. 6x9 PAPERBACK. ILLUSTRATED. BIBLIOGRAPHY. INDEX. $18.95. CODE: LLEE

THE ORION PROPHECY
Egyptian & Mayan Prophecies on the Cataclysm of 2012
by Patrick Geryl and Gino Ratinckx

In the year 2012 the Earth awaits a super catastrophe: its magnetic field reverse in one go. Phenomenal earthquakes and tidal waves will completely destroy our civilization. Europe and North America will shift thousands of kilometers northwards into polar climes. Nearly everyone will perish in the apocalyptic happenings. These dire predictions stem from the Mayans and Egyptians—descendants of the legendary Atlantis. The Atlanteans had highly evolved astronomical knowledge and were able to exactly predict the previous world-wide flood in 9792 BC. They built tens of thousands of boats and escaped to South America and Egypt. In the year 2012 Venus, Orion and several others stars will take the same 'code-positions' as in 9792 BC! For thousands of years historical sources have told of a forgotten time capsule of ancient wisdom located in a mythical labyrinth of secret chambers filled with artifacts and documents from the previous flood. We desperately need this information now—and this book gives one possible location.
324 PAGES. 6x9 PAPERBACK. ILLUSTRATED. BIBLIOGRAPHY. $16.95. CODE: ORP

ALTAI-HIMALAYA
A Travel Diary
by Nicholas Roerich

Nicholas Roerich's classic 1929 mystic travel book is back in print in this deluxe paperback edition. The famous Russian-American explorer's expedition through Sinkiang, Altai-Mongolia and Tibet from 1924 to 1928 is chronicled in 12 chapters and reproductions of Roerich's inspiring paintings. Roerich's "Travel Diary" style incorporates various mysteries and mystical arts of Central Asia including such arcane topics as the hidden city of Shambala, Agartha, more. Roerich is recognized as one of the great artists of this century and the book is richly illustrated with his original drawings.
407 PAGES. 6x9 PAPERBACK. ILLUSTRATED. $18.95. CODE: AHIM

24 hour credit card orders—call: 815-253-6390 fax: 815-253-6300
email: auphq@frontiernet.net   www.adventuresunlimitedpress.com   www.wexclub.com

One Adventure Place
P.O. Box 74
Kempton, Illinois 60946
United States of America
•Tel.: 1-800-718-4514 or 815-253-6390
•Fax: 815-253-6300
Email: auphq@frontiernet.net
http://www.adventuresunlimitedpress.com
or www.adventuresunlimited.nl

10% Discount when you order 3 or more items!

ORDERING INSTRUCTIONS

✓ Remit by USD$ Check, Money Order or Credit Card
✓ Visa, Master Card, Discover & AmEx Accepted
✓ Prices May Change Without Notice
✓ 10% Discount for 3 or more Items

SHIPPING CHARGES

United States

✓ Postal Book Rate { $3.00 First Item / 50¢ Each Additional Item
✓ Priority Mail { $4.50 First Item / $2.00 Each Additional Item
✓ UPS { $5.00 First Item / $1.50 Each Additional Item
   NOTE: UPS Delivery Available to Mainland USA Only

Canada

✓ Postal Book Rate { $6.00 First Item / $2.00 Each Additional Item
✓ Postal Air Mail { $8.00 First Item / $2.50 Each Additional Item
✓ Personal Checks or Bank Drafts MUST BE
✓ USD$ and Drawn on a US Bank / Canadian Postal Money Orders in US$ OK
✓ Payment MUST BE US$

All Other Countries

✓ Surface Delivery { $10.00 First Item / $4.00 Each Additional Item
✓ Postal Air Mail { $14.00 First Item / $5.00 Each Additional Item
✓ Checks and Money Orders MUST BE US$
   and Drawn on a US Bank or branch.
✓ Payment by credit card preferred!

SPECIAL NOTES

✓ RETAILERS: Standard Discounts Available
✓ BACKORDERS: We Backorder all Out-of-
   Stock Items Unless Otherwise Requested
✓ PRO FORMA INVOICES: Available on Request
✓ VIDEOS: NTSC Mode Only. Replacement only.
✓ For PAL mode videos contact our other offices:

European Office:
Adventures Unlimited, Pannewal 22,
Enkhuizen, 1602 KS, The Netherlands
http: www.adventuresunlimited.nl
Check Us Out Online at:
www.adventuresunlimitedpress.com

Please check: ☑

☐ This is my first order   ☐ I have ordered before   ☐ This is a new address

Name
Address
City
State/Province   Postal Code
Country
Phone day   Evening
Fax   Email

Item Code	Item Description	Price	Qty	Total

Please check: ☑

☐ Postal-Surface
☐ Postal-Air Mail (Priority in USA)
☐ UPS (Mainland USA only)

Subtotal ➡
Less Discount-10% for 3 or more items ➡
Balance ➡
Illinois Residents 6.25% Sales Tax ➡
Previous Credit ➡
Shipping ➡
Total (check/MO in USD$ only) ➡

☐ Visa/MasterCard/Discover/Amex
Card Number
Expiration Date

10% Discount When You Order 3 or More Items!

Comments & Suggestions	Share Our Catalog with a Friend